Channel your energies and redirect your life style for success!

'We can influence our destiny. We have the choice to be special. . . . I want to share my own secrets with you so that *you* too can be a winner . . . I believe everybody can be wealthy and successful if they put their minds to it.'

G000048784

Uri Geller

Uri Geller's
Fortune Secrets

SPHERE BOOKS LIMITED

First published in Great Britain by
Sphere Books Ltd 1987
27 Wrights Lane, London W8 5TZ
Copyright © Uri Geller and John Lisners 1986

Excerpts from *The Geller Papers*, edited by
Charles Panati, copyright © 1976 by
Charles Panati, are reprinted by permission
of Houghton Mifflin Company and
Curtis Brown Associates Ltd.
Material from *The Metal Benders* by Professor
John Hasted is quoted by kind permission
of Routledge & Kegan Paul.

TRADE
MARK

Set in Trump
by The Word Factory Limited, Rossendale, Lancashire

Printed in Great Britain by
Richard Clay Ltd, Bungay, Suffolk

'Based on preliminary investigations of Uri Geller, I cannot establish fraud. The powers of this man are a phenomenon which theoretical physics cannot yet explain'

Dr Friedbert Karger (Max Planck Institute for Plasma Physics, Munich)

'The Geller Effect is one of those "para" phenomena which changed the world of physics. What the most outstanding physicists of the last decades of this century could grasp only as theoretical implication, Uri brought it as fact into everyday life'

Dr Walter A. Frank (Bonn University, Bonn)

'Metal objects were bent or divided by Geller in circumstances such as to prove conclusively that the phenomena were genuine and para-normal'

Dr A.R.G. Owen (New Horizons Research Foundation, Toronto, Canada)

'There is no logical explanation for what Geller did here, but I don't think logic is what necessarily makes new in-roads in science'

Dr Thomas Coohill, (Western Kentucky University, Physics Dept, Bowling Green)

'Geller has bent my ring in the palm of my hand without ever touching it. Personally, I have no scientific explanation for the phenomena'

Wernher von Braun, (NASA scientist)

'The Geller method of breaking steel is unlike anything described in the [Metallurgical] literature, from fatigue fractures −195 degrees to brittle fractures +600 degrees Centigrade . . . Why is metal bending important? Simply because we do not understand it'

Professor John B. Hasted (Birkbeck College, University of London)

'The evidence based on metallurgical analysis of fractured surfaces [produced by Geller] indicates that a paranormal influence must have been operative in the formation of the fractures'
> Dr Wilbur Franklin (Physics Department, Kent State University)

'As a result of Geller's success in this experimental period, we consider that he has demonstrated his paranormal perceptual ability in a convincing and unambiguous manner' (The results of these experiments were published in the respected British journal *Nature*, Volume 251, No. 5476)
> Dr Harold Puthoff and Russell Targ (Stanford Research Institute)

'The bends in metal objects [made by Geller] could not have been made by ordinary manual means'
> Dr Albert Ducrocq (Telementry Laboratory, Foch Hospital, Suren, France)

'Geller altered the lattice structure of a metal alloy in a way that cannot be duplicated. There is no present scientific explanation as to how he did this' (This is the first research related to parapsychology conducted at a US Government facility to have been released for publication by the US Department of Defense)
> Eldon Byrd (US Naval Surface Weapons Center, Maryland)

'I have failed to conceive of any means of deception in the static PK tests with Geller, nor have magicians I have consulted'
> William E. Cox (Institute of Parapsychology, Durham, North Carolina)

When you read this book
I suggest you have a pen
or pencil ready.
Note down any thoughts or
ideas you have. They will
be useful to you.

The PSI-force in all of us

If I could write a book exposing myself as a fraud and a charlatan I would readily do so. Because I know that such a book would be another best seller. For millions of people around the world would love to know if I really fooled the Pentagon or scientists at The Stanford Research Institute, and the University of London. But unfortunately I cannot do this because the things that have happened to me, and the things that may very well happen to you after reading this book, are *real*.

No magic or illusion was involved when hundreds of amazed television viewers watched their own spoons bend and watches mend while my face dominated their TV screens. How was I able to do it from a television studio? As much as I would like to claim the credit, the truth of the matter is that it was not me projecting my powers. It was *you* the viewer using your hidden powers without even realising it. *You* brought your broken clocks back to life. *You* made the family silver twist and curl like spaghetti. My role was that of an agent who triggered off powers you did not know existed.

That is what I call the PSI-FORCE and it is there just waiting to be used for whatever legitimate purpose you require. I will teach you how to take advantage of that force within you and also share with you the secrets of my own powers. Why? Because I want everyone to be as content and as secure and as happy as I am. PSI-FORCE has granted me the oppotunity of making powerful friends. It has introduced me to princes, presidents and prime ministers, given me homes in four countries and made me a multi-millionaire. I believe it can do the same for you.

A funny thing happened to me

Most of us do not question unusual incidents which take place in our lives unless their effects have had a devastating influence. Even then, we may only record the event in our minds without delving too deeply into the reasons. We will certainly discuss it with friends, remark on its unusual nature and put it all down to coincidence or that often used phrase: 'a funny thing happened to me.'

Scientists love to use the word 'coincidence.' It can save a lot of embarrassing questions which they might otherwise need to explain. Questions to which they have no answers. Let me give you an example. A group of scientists want to test Uri Geller. They ask me to sit on a chair in an otherwise empty room. Then they march in ten different people, one after the other. As each person comes into the room they are asked to draw in their minds a picture of a simple object. I am asked what that object is and on each occasion I correctly describe the mental image they have projected. Nearly all the scientists present are impressed with the results but simply describe the proceedings as 'an amazing coincidence.' One of their number, however, is not so sure that it was a coincidence. He is more open-minded than the others and believes there are deeper explanations involved which as yet we know little about. He believes in the tremendous power of the mind and its capacity to project and receive images – telepathy.

Now add up *all* the 'funny things' that have happened to you in you life; things for which you never sought an explanation. Recall those occasions when you were thinking about someone and that person suddenly telephoned you. 'That's funny, I was just thinking about you.' Isn't that what you've said a hundred times? More? Or again, someone, perhaps a friend or relative was on your mind and, what a coincidence, you suddenly meet that person in the supermarket or at the cinema. Coincidence? Perhaps, jokingly you've also said: 'I must be psychic.' Well, let me tell you – you are.

What you have repeatedly done over the years, without even realising it, is to communicate by means of mental telepathy. Sometimes you have acted as the receiver, other times you have been the transmitter. And the closer you have been to the other party, the stronger the signals each of you received. You have only to study the remarkable extent of unspoken communication between identical twins to realise how powerful the telepathic process can be. Identical twins have been known to experience each other's joy and grief – even when they are hundreds of miles apart.

Now let me tell you of a tragic event that happened in America. This story was recorded by parapsychologists or PSI researchers, scientists whose research includes the study of inexplicable occurrences (the paranormal). For them, this story asked more questions than it answered. It is what I call a 'scientific frightener' because it takes us into unknown waters and inquires whether or not there are qualities in humans which might relate to time and space and suggests there is something in us that will continue, even after we die.

Sadly, it involved a lady in Brooklyn, New York,

whose son was a fighter pilot in the United States Air Force serving in Korea. The woman was going about her normal household chores when she heard the front doorbell ring. She had no idea who it could be but was so shocked on answering the call that she has never quite fully recovered from the consequences. For the person at the door was her son, proudly standing there in his uniform and impatient to greet his mother. Despite her surprise at seeing him – after all, she believed he was still in Korea – she was overwhelmed with excitement and the pair embraced warmly and lovingly. But then, just as mysteriously as he had appeared, he vanished again. Numbed by the event, his mother fainted at the spot where the reunion took place and was revived by a neighbour to whom she immediately related this story. Both the mother and neighbour were perplexed by the 'apparition' until a few hours later when the pilot's mother was informed by the US Air Force that her son had been killed while on manoeuvres in Korea.

I am convinced many of us have had similar experiences but have been reluctant to talk about them. How would you explain the airman's appearance? Would you say it was chance, communication with the dead – clairvoyance, telepathy, precognition, or even astral projection? I have an open mind which would accept many of the above possibilities. But to my mind, the least possible of these alternatives is chance. I do not believe it was chance because I understand the amazing powers our minds are capable of generating. As for the pilot's mother, she was sure from that day on that her son wanted to communicate with her from the grave. I would suggest another explanation. Because of the strong bond that existed between mother and son, she received his thought signals when he died but she wanted to avoid the truth of the tragedy by imagining that he had returned safely.

Whichever explanation we give, or you decide on yourself, the fact remains there was *communication* over a distance of thousands of miles. Don't ever think that believing something like this will class you as a 'nutter.' That great writer and philosopher, Arthur Koestler, a man with whom I spent many long hours before his death, left the bulk of his estate to a British University for psychic research. I will talk about Arthur in later chapters but it is important to note that a man who enjoyed an international reputation as a writer, scientist, and philosopher, should believe in powers beyond normal mental abilities. He was fascinated by what he called 'out of the blue phenomena' – levitation, ESP, telepathy, and precognition. Moments before he died, he left a suicide note in which he expressed 'timid hopes for a depersonalised after-life beyond due confines of space, time and matter, and beyond the limits of our comprehension.' No one who knew this eminent thinker would ever suggest *he* was a nut!

If twenty years ago I had told someone, as I then believed, that it would be possible to communicate by telepathy with a man on the moon, I would probably have been asked to accompany four white-coated gentlemen to the nearest asylum. But now scientists are taking claims like this seriously. Because it has been done! The sixth American on the moon, astronaut Dr Edgar Mitchell, a respected scientist in his own right, revealed that he had successfully transmitted telepathic messages from the moon. As a result of his interest in PSI he became a full-time researcher after quitting the space programme. Like me, he believes that psychic experiences can benefit each and every one of us if these powers are properly developed and employed. They are not there to be used as a prop, nor are they something of a mystery. They are there to be developed, just like an arm or a leg or the fingers of a hand. We all possess them. The only difference is that very few of us use them.

The PSI factors

Most people who believe in the existence of a god or a superior force have excellent prospects for developing PSI power. It is only the total cynic who believes in nothing but himself and will not acknowledge the possibility of a greater power or superior being. That person will be limited by his own ignorance. Fortunately, there are very few of those smug, self-sufficient souls around. From my own observations, I tend not to believe in these obstinate agnostics. As much as they protest, they can often turn to the 'unknown' in times of need. I have been on battlefields and heard these non-believers cry out for help: 'God, if there is a God, help me!' Such a cry does not pay lip service to any one particular religion. But if the plea is heard then it does tend to drastically change the person's viewpoint.

Now if you are a doubting Thomas, take this appeal for help one step further. If you actually believe a force has helped you in a time of need, why not call on that same force when you are *not* in trouble but want to enhance the quality of your existence and explore the opportunities life has to offer? The applications are countless and the

6

opportunities unlimited. You have only to believe that it *can* be done.

PSI-FORCE can be of continuing benefit to you in your daily life. It will help you to excel in sport, outsmart your boss, win at games, make friends, attract the opposite sex, be a good lover, overcome illness and depression, come to terms with death or disaster, be a financial success, and, above all, be happy and content.

But you must learn how to channel it your way. Remember that it *is* a force and wherever there is a force, there must be a proper outlet as otherwise its effect can be misdirected. What I am saying is that you need to direct that special PSI-FORCE through a practical channel to maximise the advantage it will bring to you. And this is what I will be teaching you in the subsequent chapters of this book. How to get the *best* out of *your* particular talent using that dynamic force that is in you, just waiting to be awakened, sharpened and properly and practically channelled for your benefit. And just as I asked millions of television viewers to let me know if their clocks started again when they joined me in this mind over matter exercise, so I am also asking you, when you have finished this book and realised the benefits, to let me know. Don't keep it to yourself, share it with your friends. Spread happiness around as I am trying to do. Send a short letter to my publishers. I cannot promise to answer all your letters because I know there will be so many that it will be an impossible task. But I am convinced that for the millions who will read this book, their life may never again be the same.

Let's look at different aspects of PSI. If we accept that inexplicable things happen in our lives then we must not scoff at ideas that initially seem 'far out' or that appear totally beyond our comprehension. But please, do keep an open mind. Remember that what might have been regarded as science fiction thirty years ago is commonplace today. As this is a practical book, I will not delve too deeply into what some people might regard as science fiction or metaphysical concepts. But it is just as well to have a basic idea of the wonderful things which will happen in the future and excite generations to come. Take for example, the use to which the human mind could be put during an international conflict. It may sound as if this should belong to sci-fiction but I can assure you that governments of various countries have already shown more than a passing interest in the paranormal and are holding secret tests into PSI-FORCE.

The government mandarins would love to be able to read the minds of their opposite numbers. They would love to interfere with enemy computers using PSI-FORCE rather than hi-tech. I do not say this lightly, because I have been asked to do these very things by high ranking members of foreign governments.

The word 'psychic' is less frequently used these days for one very good reason. It tended to be met with scepticism and acquired a stigma because of charlatans who claimed false powers. Today it is being replaced with words like PSI or 'paranormal' because of the wider acceptability of its existence. PSI is explained as a phenomenon which appears to contradict the laws of natural science.

For example, if an object is placed on a table at point A but we want that object to be at a different spot twenty centimeters away on the same table, at point B, we will either have to pick it up or push it or tilt the table so it slides to point B. How that object moved from point A to point B can then be explained in scientific terms. It was moved by a physical force. But what if the object moved from one point to the other through PSI-FORCE? What if someone *willed* that object to move and it did so without anyone exerting a physical force? Then the only explanation applying would be the phenomena of 'psychokinesis': the mind influencing matter and so contradicting the laws of natural science.

To some people, psychokinesis comes very naturally and easily, often embarrassing the initiator of the force. I have been in a room where objects have literally flown about and come crashing down, scaring everyone present. This phenomenon also brings us into the area of the poltergeist – a terrible psychic beast who appears generally when children are present and throws things at random around the room as well as showing off his powers of levitation. It is also a very good example of what could be a useful force being wasted and made dangerous through lack of proper control. But just think if you *could* control those objects.

Have you ever carelessly thrown a scrap of rolled up paper into a narrow dustbin from a distance of several yards and scored a direct hit? Did it surprise you? Well, if it did not surprise you, try a little test and see how many times out of ten you could repeat that score. Often, when we are not really trying, we find we have amazing accuracy in judgement. I believe that the forces at work are related to psychokinesis. You may not be a very good shot but your mind has willed that piece of paper or object you are throwing to hit the target. Now perhaps you can understand why sports writers wax eloquent about the 'magical' qualities of ball players. What they are really describing is the player's highly developed PSI-FORCE – practically combined with sound physical prowess.

Nearly every day a superhuman feat is recorded somewhere in the world. A man falls out of an aeroplane and survives, a mother prises open the jaws of a ten foot long killer shark and saves her young daughter. These are astounding acts of human will power achieving the impossible. PSI-FORCE.

When I was in the Amazon jungle I witnessed the amazing skill of a local native, an Amerindian. He was an old man whose fame for hunting was widespread. He wore scant clothing and his prized possession was a bamboo blow pipe into which he would place poison arrows and kill small prey for food. He was also very religious, having been partly taught traditional religion by Christian missionaries which his tribe had then adapted into their own religion, and whose god was called 'Ibilibin' – 'I believe in'. This little man did not impress me at first with his skill. I thought, like those present, that it was a normal everyday skill which he had learned and which members of his tribe had to rely on for their very existence. It was only when I learned that the man was *blind* that I became aware of the magnitude of PSI-FORCE in the human race. Have you not admired the way in which a blind person will walk across busy roads, down steps, and stop at the edge of a bank or road? Some people describe this behaviour as a sixth sense. The description is immaterial. What that person possesses is a highly developed and practical form of PSI.

Dowsing is another highly developed form of PSI. On my visit to Australia, I was surprised at the number of people who believed in this art. The reason, of course, was need. Australia has some of the most arid countryside in the world and they

10

depend on drilling for bore water. And even the most down to earth 'cocky' (a name given to outback farmers) would think nothing of calling in an expert with a Y-shaped twig to find water. But try and explain to that farmer that this was a manifestation of the paranormal and he will very smartly tell you where to take your 'mumbo jumbo.' Fortunately, as I have said, that attitude is dying out and I, in fact, had a very profitable time dowsing for gold with a down-under company.

The best family doctors, though they will probably be the last to admit it, are also natural healers. A lot of them would probably be just as effective in curing many ailments whether they had passed their examinations at a medical school or not, or even, for that fact, ever attended medical school. Unfortunately, a number of general practitioners who have subscribed to this theory are singled out as being a little odd or eccentric. They are also scared of the term 'spiritual healing' which basically means that PSI-FORCE is used to diagnose and treat illness.

I know of an English policeman who became a marvellous healer in the south-west of England. He resigned from the police force because so many police came to him with their ailments that he had no time to man his beat. He could diagnose illnesses within seconds and then cure them just as quickly by putting his hands over the person's head and running them down the patient's spine. Although the power of healing is stronger in some than in others, it can be developed and self-healing has become a widespread and much practised art.

Another form of PSI which has helped many people face the inevitable conclusion of death is the out-of-the-body (or near death) experience and the possibility of reincarnation. Those who have faced or are facing death, have found comfort and an inner happiness by drawing on the experiences of those very special people who have been pronounced clinically dead but were then later revived.

When the British actress Pat Phoenix was dying of cancer, her mental suffering was greatly eased on hearing stories of life after death and the experiences of those close to her who had entered the twilight world but then returned. So too were Rock Hudson's last days lightened.

Much research has been done in this field and most of it has pointed to a happier existence hereafter. The out-of-the-body experience, I might add, is not confined to the above category of person but also takes place in perfectly healthy people. It is a form of astral travel – the psychic body leaves the physical body. It is quite an eerie yet somehow exciting experience to look down at your body knowing you are out of it. How wonderful it would be if we could all travel within an instant to see our friends who live on the other side of the world. It's also a lot cheaper than air travel!

How often have you walked into a room or some other place and known that you have been there before? I would be very surprised if the reader of this book has not experienced the phenomena of déjà vu, the 'I've been here before' syndrome. One possible explanation for this is that you have precognition. You have had a view of the future and when your physical body then experiences what your telepathic mind has already seen, you think you have been there before. I consider that our mind has such a strong telepathic energy wave that it can travel distances faster than the speed of light. Imagine if you could control that? You would be barred from Wall Street and the stock exchanges in Tokyo, Frankfurt and the City of London as well as every race-track and casino in the world. But just think of the fun you would have in the meantime!

So far, I have only touched on some of the aspects of PSI which are probably familiar to you. There are many more I will talk about in the subsequent chapters, but for the moment I want you to realise, even if you did not believe in these powers before, that there must be something in them. Keep thinking back at the number of incidents in your life where you have experienced the improbable or the inexplicable. Because what we will try and do for you is to make it possible to replicate those incidents which you found pleasant and beneficial. If you achieve this, then you are beginning to channel your PSI-FORCE. But you must practise and you must be flexible and tolerant to what is happening. The PSI experience is an all-embracing one. If you shut out the possibility of one form of PSI happening, you are in danger of shutting out *all* the possibilities. An open and a receptive mind is the most essential ingredient for PSI development.

Now I want you to answer the following questions. Think about them and be honest with yourself. Answer these questions with either: 'Yes' or 'Not sure' or 'No.'

1. Do you believe that psychic healing really works?
2. Have your dreams sometimes come true?
3. Do you believe in the existence of a God?
4. Do you think telepathy between people is possible?
5. Do you sometimes look at the Bible for inspiration?
6. Do you think there is life after death?

7. Have you ever been to a seance?
8. Would you be scared by prophecies of death?
9. Do you consider it possible for us to be visited by aliens from another planet?
10. Do you think ESP/telepathy is really possible?
11. Do you think ghosts or apparitions will ever be scientifically documented?
12. Have you ever consulted a clairvoyant?
13. Do you often read astrological predictions?
14. Have you experienced strange happenings that have been more than coincidence?
15. Do you consider yourself to have psychic powers?

Scoring Give yourself 2 points for each 'Yes' answer, 1 point for each 'Not sure' answer and 0 points for each 'No' answer. Then add up your total score.

A score of 14 or more indicates that you *are* interested in the possibility of psychic phenomena. At least you are open-minded about the claims of the paranormal, if not actually involved.

A score of 20 or more suggests that you are a true believer. You are the sort of person who experiences the mystical side of things. Apart from being broader than average, your life experiences are likely to be more intense. For you, falling in love would be an earth shattering experience.

High scorers on this scale are more likely to demonstrate psychic ability when put to the test. Conversely, very low scorers have been found to score less than they would by chance.

If you have scored less than 14, you have not yet opened your mind to the possibility of PSI phenomena. But do not give up. The fact that you have started reading this book is a good sign that you are now willing to examine the subject and give it a try.

But high or low, if you believe in the possibility, then *you* are with me all the way and I will teach you everything I know. Let's get to work straightaway and use our combined powers to give you a new and better understanding of life! We share the same talents and beliefs. *You* have only to develop yours!

Destiny and dynasty

I believe that every person has a talent which can be put to good use. The problem, of course, is to identify your particular talent and make the best of it. PSI-FORCE can help you in this respect, and later in this chapter I will tell you how.

But first let me assure you that no one should ever lose hope or be demoralised if their present circumstances are such that they seem trapped and incapable of moving forwards. Furthermore, don't think that just because you weren't born with that silver spoon in your mouth, you have missed out. I am a believer in fate, but at the same time I also believe that fate and destiny are interlinked and that you *can* help to direct your destiny.

Take nature as an example: Why do you think a queen bee is special? Is it hereditary? No, all the larvae produced in a hive are the same. The young pupae which develop into queen bees are different because they are fed a diet of royal jelly in special cells and were it not for this they would be the same as any of the worker bees. Now obviously we can't all be born princes, but we can develop special qualities just like the bees if we are trained properly and fed the right information to develop our dormant talents. Not everyone can be a genius or become super-skilled, but even a little improvement is better than none and the change you undergo with even a little improvement will give you confidence to do more. And remember that humans have an extra dimension, unlike insects or animals. They have a choice. We can influence our destiny. *We* have the choice to be *special*.

So if you were not born into a happy dynasty, you can make it *your* destiny to be happy and perhaps even become privileged through developing your skills. After all, it can be far more fulfilling to know that you have made it on your own and not through accident of birth. I also want to assure you that if you are successful at creating your own destiny, then it is very likely that you will rub noses with the 'dynasty set' anyway. Who would have thought that someone from my humble background would one day attend parties thrown for princes? I do not say this to boast but only to illustrate the point that it can be done. And that all it takes is that extra knowledge, its application, and an open and receptive mind.

In other words, look on PSI-FORCE as another acquired skill. Then, if you maximise the benefits it has to offer, you will surely be head and shoulders above others who have not taken advantage of it.

And don't be frightened to discuss your PSI skills and interests with other people. Don't worry if they think you are a little strange or weird; that kind of comment is often passed about some of the most successful and distinguished people. I can also assure you that the most prestigious dynasty in the world, the Royal House of Windsor, has among its most prominent members a very strong belief in PSI. In fact, I will go so far as to say that the next King of England, if he is not already a practising spiritualist, has dabbled in spiritualism despite the adverse publicity given to his unorthodox views on life.

Prince Charles is a very spiritual person with an extremely open and receptive mind. He is willing to explore unconventional avenues despite his most conventional position in public life. The Prince's willingness to embrace new ideas and accept cosmic forces means that he would be a very good candidate to perform feats like metal bending and telepathy.

Prince Charles believes in the search for happiness and tranquillity through the inner self. When he spoke to Canadian lumberjacks and local business people in May 1986, his words were quoted around the world. He told a crowd of thousands in the heart of British Columbia: 'I rather feel that deep in the soul of mankind there is a reflection as on the surface of a mirror, of a mirror-calm lake, of the beauty and harmony of the universe. But so often that reflection is obscured and ruffled by unaccountable storms. So much depends, I think, on how each one of us is introduced to and is made aware of that reflection within us. I believe we have a duty to our children to try to develop this awareness, for it seems to me that it is only through the outer manifestation of that reflection, that we can ever hope to attain the kind of peace in this world for which we yearn. We must try if we can to make living into an art itself although it will always remain a tremendous struggle.'

Prince Charles is known to have been greatly influenced by Sir Laurens van der Post. Sir Laurens, an octogenarian, and the young heir to the throne, have a deep mystical relationship. It is like a rich, grandfather-grandson relationship and extraordinarily important to both; especially to Charles after IRA terrorists savagely murdered his beloved 'uncle', the elder statesman, Lord Louis Mountbatten.

Sir Laurens, a South African writer and philosopher, lives in London. Pictures of the Prince and paintings by him abound in the old man's apartment. Sir Laurens is a man with a keen interest in Eastern religions, particularly Buddhism; and not only that, but physics and psychology are also their meeting point. Of his disciple the Prince, the guru says that Charles thinks for himself and doesn't need his 'master' to show him the way.

Charles, says Sir Laurens, has the Greek idea of being a whole man. And the great thing is that the Prince of Wales is a searcher, looking for answers still far from clear to man. Indeed, the spiritual self is not the Prince's only interest. He is also a great believer in alternative medicine and in faith healing, a subject he discussed at length with Dr Mervyn Stockwood, the former Bishop of a London diocese. He met the bishop through his second cousin, Princess Alexandra, whose husband, Angus Ogilvy, often consulted faith healers because of a painful back ailment.

The Prince is not concerned with what others think of his views. He has said: 'People often remain silent about what they really think in case everyone should think they are mad. But when someone in my position says, "I think there is something in that," many people who have remained silent admit to feeling the same way.'

He also said: 'We are a left brain society. We concentrate on organising the denial of the intuitive right half of the brain. To me it is very interesting to see how primitive societies are the whole time subconsciously far more aware of their instinctive relationship with people and things around them than we are in the so-called civilised world. I believe instinct, sensitivity, call it what you will, is enormously important.'

Perhaps we should all take a leaf out of his book. For it was also Prince Charles who upset the British

Medical Association by challenging them to discover alternative medicine and begging them to keep an open mind to the unconventional. In 1982 he told their distinguished gathering: 'One of the less attractive traits of various professional bodies is the deeply ingrained suspicion and downright hostility which can exist towards anything unorthodox. I suppose it is inevitable that something which is different should arouse strong feelings on the part of the majority whose conventional wisdom is being challenged. I suppose too, that human nature is such that we are frequently prevented from seeing that what is taken for today's unorthodoxy is probably going to be tomorrow's convention.'

Without a doubt, PSI has got the royal seal of approval! There have been constant reports that Prince Charles has tried through spiritual means to contact his favourite uncle, Lord Dickie Mountbatten, who himself had been interested in PSI, as indeed have many other members of the British royal family. The Queen has been to spiritual healers and the family history has recorded many incidents involving psychic phenomena. Queen Victoria apparently held seances in Buckingham Palace and contacted her dear departed husband Albert through a Scottish medium called John Brown. The Queen Mother later followed suit and contacted her dead husband King George VI through Lillian Bailey, a well-known medium. Ghosts have been seen on many occasions and there have been many instances of clairvoyance and telepathy.

The Queen is a very religious person and a strong believer in cosmic order and destiny. Because of her strong dynastic feelings she feels it is her duty to continue as monarch rather than hand over to her eldest son.

Prince Charles will not wear the mantle of king lightly but he will wear it with profound honesty and humanity. And the reason for this is the spiritual man within him. He is sincere and caring and in another life it is quite conceivable that he would have fully immersed himself in the pursuit of PSI research or have been a spiritualist or a faith healer of great repute. I sense in him a special aura that could be developed to a great degree. He believes in the power of PSI-FORCE and wants to use it for the greater public good. He wants to see his subjects help themselves through an inner belief in their own powers. That is why he is so concerned with community projects around Britain and the world. He does not believe money alone will solve people's problems but that they have to learn to respect their own inner forces and utilise these forces for their benefit. And even though he has through birth achieved what most people could only dream of having, he is intent on developing his PSI powers to find an inner happiness just like any one of us.

But I also believe that he will use PSI power when he becomes king and that he will be an extremely popular and much loved monarch as a result. Many of his decisions will not be made without reference to his psychic self. He will try and use precognition, telepathy, and psychic projection, all of which he is still developing and will continue to develop throughout his life.

Charles has a refreshing, open mind. Cautiously, in an interview with Sir Alistair Burnett of Britain's Independent Television News, the Prince remarked: 'I am not interested in the occult, or dabbling in black magic or any of these kind of things or, for that matter, strange forms of mysticism. But,' he declared, 'I am purely interested in being open-minded.' And indeed he is. For I know of a secret meeting which Charles had at his home in Kensington Palace with a leading British scientist. Fascinated, the Prince discussed metal bending and was shown spoons bent by children.

Those glamorous young royals, the Duke and Duchess of York also have a great interest in PSI. Before their wedding, I was invited to a party in London at which they were guests of honour and word was passed to me that Prince Andrew and Sarah Ferguson would love to meet me. Without further ado, the royal couple were steered in my direction and we were introduced. I immediately sensed that Prince Andrew wanted to see me do something with my powers and I asked the Prince: "Would you like me to bend a spoon for you?"

Andrew said he would be delighted to watch me do just that and hauled Sarah to his side to make sure she did not miss the event.

I did not want to steal the limelight at the party so I asked if we could do it away from the main body of those present. David Frost, who had organised the evening, took us into his kitchen and gave me one of the family's silver spoons. Although they were both smiling, neither Andrew nor Sarah could take their eyes off my fingers as I gently stroked the spoon and willed it to bend. They were not disappointed. Once the spoon began bending it did not stop. It even continued bending when I gave it to Sarah to hold. Prince Andrew then took it from her and waved it around at the party to show everybody what had happened.

Later, as a wedding gift, I sent the couple a silver spoon given to my son Daniel when he was born. As such, it was a very special gift. It also had further significance in as much as I bent the spoon at the very precise second that Andrew slipped the wedding ring on to Sarah's finger. Obviously it meant something to the Duke and Duchess as well, because some weeks later I received a letter from Buckingham Palace dated August 11, 1986. It said: 'Dear Uri, we were absolutely delighted to receive your wedding gift of the silver spoon bent on our wedding day. It is very kind of you to send us such a lovely present, which will be greatly treasured, and we much appreciate your good wishes at this very happy time. Yours sincerely, Andrew and Sarah.'

I sometimes wonder if the royal family receives an added PSI boost through their ability to fly aeroplanes. Experiments have been conducted to show that fighter pilots have a highly developed sense of ESP. Despite the technological advances in aeronautics, you have still to rely on intuition and feeling when flying. Your senses are trained to be more alert than they would be otherwise. Combat pilots have often spoken about feeling the presence of the enemy before actually seeing them.

But there is another aspect, a more metaphysical one that can pervade your mind when flying in a twilight zone. I can assure you, if you have not already experienced it, that it can be a most edifying and humbling experience. The might of the universe suddenly makes its magnificent presence felt. New horizons are opened and if you allow your feelings to take over, you can imagine that you are part of the universe, riding along on an astral path. Try it sometime when you next go on a foreign trip or holiday and you are flying in a semi-light or on a very starry night. Look out of the window and imagine you are far from planet earth. You will be amazed at the clarity of your mind and the different approach you use in questioning your very being in this expanded universe to which you now belong. Try it when you get back to earth too. Do it by standing alone in an empty field at night and watch the stars and universe. That will very quickly and effectively put you in touch with the cosmos. It is also a marvellous way to relax all your senses. And it is bound to help you review your current lifestyle by giving you a better or different perspective of yourself.

I can never stress strongly enough the importance of PSI and I hope from having read the above you will agree that if there was nothing in it then the most important family in the world would not bother pursuing it. Why should they? Haven't they got everything? Money, breeding, they are at the pinnacle of society, they have a lifestyle which millions envy. Nevertheless, they do pursue it because it is a gift that must be developed and which *you* have as much access to as they do! After all, they still have to make constant decisions in their life. They are still prone to the same illnesses as other people and they can still be unhappy and depressed, no matter what their breeding.

The psychic mirror

How do you see yourself? How often do you sit back and take a long hard look at *you*? A useful exercise which I recommend to everyone who wants to learn more about their PSI, is the mirror exercise. Make sure you are alone in the room, perform a few simple exercises to help you relax, and then take a long look at yourself in the mirror, possibly a full-length one. Scan your whole body from top to toe and then concentrate on your face. Look at your forehead, your eyes, your nose and mouth and chin. After a while, it may seem to you that you are looking at a stranger. That's good. That is how you should look at yourself. Now try and determine how you feel about that stranger. What do you like or dislike about the person you are looking at? What can you see behind the physical mask? Can you read anything into those eyes? What colour are they? What colour is the hair? Really dissect the face you see in front of you. Now take a notebook and sit down and list everything you feel and see. What about the clothes? Do you like them? It does not matter in what order you list your impressions but make sure that you list both what you *see* and what you *feel* about the image in front of you. I guarantee that you will be surprised by the amount of 'feeling' you get from this image.

When you have finished writing, return once more to the mirror and ask yourself if what you have surmised about the reflected you is likely to be the same impression others have. Look at yourself and try and imagine that you are now one of your close friends looking at you. What vibes are you getting? What do you feel about the general appearance of the person in front of you? Again, I want you to write down all these feelings. Perhaps even record them on to a tape recorder and afterwards transcribe them. This is an important process in self discovery and realisation. You are letting your PSI do much of the work for you without even realising it until you see the results.

But you must also be positive. It is no good saying 'I hate what I see'; try and see the good points as well as the bad points. Remember the ultimate aim is to improve yourself and to be happier living with and understanding yourself and your motivations. Play out different roles in front of the mirror. Put on make-up, wash your hair and imagine you have just played a part in a film and are being interviewed on television. You want to come across to the public so you are putting your best side forward.

Another mirror exercise can usefully be done with a

friend. Explain to your friend or partner that you are trying to assess yourself and that part of the exercise involves seeing yourself as others see you. Convince him or her that it would be a good idea to do the same so you can exchange notes. But don't tell each other before you do the mirror test what you feel about each other. Get your friend to write down the impressions he or she gets of you, and you do exactly the same. But don't tell each other what they are. Then when you have both completed the exercise, compare notes. Be brutally frank with each other and you are bound to discover things you never imagined about yourself.

You can also perform PSI tests together. Tell your partner or friend to think about the strongest impression that comes to mind about you. See if you can guess what he or she is thinking. Ask them to picture in their minds a colour and see if you can name it. I will go further into PSI tests and exercises you can perform in the next chapter but it will be helpful to get into practise as soon as possible.

I often play 'guessing games' with my brother-in-law, Shipi. If, for instance, we are on a motorway, we will see who can correctly predict the number of red cars which will pass us in the next ten minutes. Alternatively we will try and predict the make of cars we will see during a space of ten or fifteen minutes. These are simple games but they all help to sharpen your PSI senses and it is fun doing them with someone you like.

But the mirror test is important. It is the beginning of the road which will take you along the path of PSI realisation and fulfilment. And the first step is to know all about your physical self and your PSI-self. Ask yourself the following questions:

1. Are you generally happy?
2. If not, what do you think is the reason?
3. Is there anything that could be done about it?
4. Are you doing what you really want to do?
5. Would you rather have another job?
6. Is it possible to get another job?
7. Are you religious or do you have basic beliefs?
8. How strong are those beliefs?
9. What is your attitude to family, to friends, to work?
10. Are you ambitious?
11. Do you have a satisfactory sex life?
12. Do you get on with people of other races?
13. Do you have high or low self esteem?
14. What do you think others think of you?
15. How could you improve your situation, if at all?
16. Are you happy with your appearance?
17. Could you improve your looks?
18. If you could be someone else who would you most like to be?
19. If you believed in reincarnation, what would you like to come back as?
20. What is your favourite animal?
21. Who do you think has influenced you more than anyone else?
22. Given the chance, would you like your life to have been different?
23. Do you think you have been hard done by in life?
24. Do you think that with positive thought you could overcome your disadvantages?
25. What do you consider to be your strengths?
26. What are your weaknesses?
27. How could you improve on them?
28. What natural talents do you think you have?

29. Could you improve your health in any way?
30. How would you describe yourself in an objective report?

Having thought about the above questions, determine for yourself if your personality type is outgoing, sociable and generally happy (extrovert) or whether you tend to be more repressed and withdrawn (introverted). Generally speaking, extrovert types are likely to be more adventurous in their life, and that includes being positive to PSI. Nevertheless, if you are introverted you can still be successful at using PSI-FORCE, providing you have a positive belief and an open mind.

Your secret chamber

Three very important ingredients of PSI-FORCE are physical exercise, relaxation, and concentration. All three factors are inter-dependent and you must try and practise all three daily, even if only for a very short time. For instance, if you have enjoyed hard physical exercise, the pleasure of relaxation will be accentuated with a good resultant effect on your mind. Concentration is then also enhanced. When first learning to concentrate, it is very important for you to be totally relaxed and there are several ways of doing this. Basically, adopt whatever physical position you find to be the most comfortable and relaxed. It could be a cushion on the floor, or lying in bed or seated in a comfortable armchair. Totally relax your body. Relax your arms, your legs, your feet. Take deep breaths and relax each muscle of each limb in turn, relax your neck and head. Tell yourself to relax each part of your body from the top of your head down to your toes, taking deep even breaths while you are doing it. While practising this make sure you are not in a bath or swimming pool in case you are too efficient at relaxing and fall asleep.

Next you must learn to shut doors on unnecessary and time consuming thoughts which can interfere with PSI energy. That means if you have niggling fears about unfinished business, or you are worrying about unpaid bills or you've had a quarrel with your partner, then your mind is not free either to concentrate on a particular aspect or alternatively to purposefully wander and explore new horizons. So what you must do is consciously say to yourself: 'I am shutting the door in my mind to all these small problems. For the moment they do not exist. I will deal with them tomorrow. I will put them in a file and close that file until I am ready.' Try it. Not only will you be able to concentrate on using your PSI powers but it will also help you sleep at night. A good night's sleep seems to sort out much of the anxiety you might have felt the evening before. You wake up refreshed and in a much fitter state to face the world. Or perhaps, by not succumbing to the problems, you have allowed your PSI to take over and it has solved the problem for you!

Another way in which you can eliminate outside worries is to concentrate on a particular object, say a flower or a medallion. Whatever it is you choose, put all your powers of concentration into that object and dismiss everything else from your mind. By concentrating on that object you do not have to think deeply about it or what it might represent. Imagine there is a television screen in your mind. Blank the screen completely and then fill it with that object. Then press the 'hold' button and transfix the image. Now concentrate on that image for several minutes before relaxing. Do this exercise several times until you have mastered the technique.

Later, you can allow other images to enter your mind which are related to the flower or medallion. Because by concentrating on a particular object you can accept other thoughts into your PSI consciousness which have been influenced by the object you are concentrating on. This will in turn prepare you for ESP and telepathy.

Many people do not realise how frequently they use this type of PSI concentration. I know of a number of friends who never need an alarm clock to wake them up no matter what time they wish to rise. Without realising it they have used their PSI alarm to wake them. The way they do it is quite simple. Before going to sleep at night, they tell themselves to wake up at a given hour and somehow their psychic clock is accurate to the second. Try it and see if it works. One of my friends who found it worked only sporadically for him changed his command structure. Instead of just telling himself to wake up at a certain hour, he taps his head on the pillow a set number of times to correspond with the hour he wants to wake. So if he wants to get up at five in the morning he will tap his head on the pillow five times. He's even worked out a system with light taps for parts of the hour. Whatever method you use, be assured it *will* work for you if you have faith in it.

Just as you can instruct your mind to wake you at a certain point in time, so too can you tell your subconscious to solve a problem while you sleep. That is a means of getting your subconscious or more accurately, your PSI-conscious to work for you. Try it now. Tell yourself that you will solve a particular problem without worrying about it and see what happens. I am sure it will work for you as it worked for me.

It is very important for you to continue assessing yourself as I have outlined and also to objectively see yourself as others see you. As you become more proficient at 'reading' yourself, you will find that you can begin to read and learn about other people just by hearing them talk and seeing their actions (body language). After all, you will find many similarities with yourself and you will be able to compare the reasons for their actions with conclusions you have already drawn from your own behaviour. What you will eventually be doing is sharpening up your 'sixth' sense – your ESP – when evaluating friends and colleagues and strangers. Whether you are buying a car, selling one, purchasing a house, being interviewed for a job, you will find the application of this power of great benefit to you.

I would also now like you to keep a special diary. Call it a PSI diary if you like. Record all the interesting things that happen to you and for which there is no apparent explanation. Eventually, you will see a pattern forming and you will find an explanation for what has taken place. But for the moment, you are still a learner so be content with just recording everything. Record your dreams. Do you dream in colour or in black and white? Do you have many dreams? Can you remember them well? Keep the diary beside your bed and if you wake up at an unsociable hour because of a dream, record it as quickly as possible. Dreams are often forgotten in a flash.

Write down all the times that you feel a psychic event has taken place in your presence. Record the times you were going to say the same thing as another person at exactly the same moment. Record your *déjà vu* experiences and the times you ran into someone you had been thinking about. If coincidences or synchronicities crop up with a particular person, you may well have a telepathic companion. In that case, start experimenting with that person. See if you can tell what each of you is thinking. Compare your choice of colours, try moving objects together. See if that person is your personality type. By working together you will heighten each other's PSI powers. Each week, add up all the strange occurrences that have taken place and record the ones that happen most frequently. That will give some clue as to where your present PSI strengths are and you can work on improving your powers. Other powers that are dormant in you may crop up only very occasionally, if at all. Don't lose heart. Work on them. Be aware they exist. Think about them. It will bring them to life.

Astrology and PSI

I am often asked if I believe in astrology and whether it is compatible with PSI. As I have said throughout this book, I have a completely open mind towards all phenomena and that includes astrology. I do believe our star signs determine part of our characters and our future and I also believe astrology can complement PSI. You may find that someone who is of the same astrological birth sign as you has many things in common and you could develop an instant rapport with that person, bringing you on to the same psychic plane. I know many people who can instantly predict the star sign of a particular person through ESP. Remember that PSI and astrology are strongly interlinked in our cosmic world.

The famous German publisher, Axel Springer, who made millions from his newspaper empire, would not make major decisions without reference to his stars. He was an avid believer in the power of PSI.

My own powers revealed

I sometimes say to myself: 'Uri, if only you were born a woman, most of the professional problems emanating from your special powers would be solved.' Let me explain. First of all, I believe in total equality of the sexes and am firmly against organisations excluding women from membership by virtue of their sex. One such organisation is the Magic Circle, a society of magicians who will not admit women to their ranks. Certain of their members who on the one hand will *not* recognise talented female magicians, insist that I, being a man, must therefore be a talented magician because by trickery, they can appear to do some of the things which I do naturally. Now, however flattering their chauvinistic thought process might seem, it does not impress me in the slightest. The logical conclusion one has to draw from their anti-woman stand is that had I been born a woman they would probably have insisted I was *not* a magician and confirmed my powers as a psychic. But as I am a man, they keep wanting me to say I am one of them. Such are the jealousies of life. And, to be fair, there are some magicians I know who tend to believe in PSI forces after some of their own experiences. However, as for the hostile sceptics, we will not waste further time with those but instead I will, in the course of this book, teach you how to deal with small and irritating pains as they arise.

My powers were evident when I was very small. The first manifestation came soon after an event that could have resulted in my death. Again, I must strictly advise everyone against trying to do the same thing as I did. Because I can assure you that the near disaster which almost befell me will not give you psychic powers but is more likely to relieve you of them for good!

My mother worked as a seamstress from our small flat in Israel. Each time she switched on the sewing machine, you could see a blue spark through a hole which was just big enough for me to insert my little finger. As a child of about five I had no idea of the dangers of electricity and poked my finger right inside the machine to see if I could feel the pretty blue spark. The results could have been devastating. As it was, I was lucky enough only to receive a tremendous electric shock which threw me on to my back. A short time after this incident, but not necessarily as a result of it, some 'strange' things began to happen.

My mother's favourite relaxation was to go out and play cards with her friends. Suddenly, I found that when she returned home I began to get print- outs from her mind. I was able to read her mind. I could tell her exactly how many card games she had won or lost and if she had been gambling with friends, I was able to predict exactly how much money she had gained or lost. But that was not all. I found I was beginning to say things seconds before she came out with them. This used to exasperate her considerably but at the time she did not know I was psychic. Then, when I was about six years old, my father gave me a watch as a present and that is when more people started becoming aware that some very odd events were taking place.

At first, my school mates were totally perplexed the way I could mentally manipulate not only my own watch but theirs as well. I could advance them, speed them up and then slow them down or make them go completely haywire. This provoked laughs against me, but very soon they acquired a respect for my talent and regarded what I did as very entertaining. I was too young at the time to know the real effect this was having on my parents but I don't think they really took too much notice. Their marriage was coming to an end and other things seemed to preoccupy them more than broken watches. It was only when spoons and other cutlery began bending or were destroyed that my father thought of inquiring into the matter by seeking professional help. He tried to find a psychiatrist for me but then thought better of it.

I can recall two 'odd' incidents from an early age. One involved a very bright light descending in my back garden when I was only about three or four years old. I do remember telling my mother about this but I don't think she believed me. As far as she was concerned it was childhood fantasy. No child, as far as she was concerned, was capable of seeing or identifying an unidentified flying object. That image, however, of the bright light, circular in shape, and so close to me, will remain with me to the end of my life. The second incident happened when I was four months old. My mother put me in a pram and placed me under a window. A British soldier across the road by the railway fired two bullets into the window. The glass shattered into millions of fragments falling all over me. I remember it vividly. I believe it may have been a 'trigger'.

I was born on 20 December, 1946, in Tel Aviv. My father, Itzhak Geller had fled Hungary six years earlier with my mother Margaret. They took different routes to reach Palestine, as Israel was then called. They were reunited in 1940 and set up home in Kerem Hateimanim, Jaffa. My mother's side of the family was from Vienna although she was born in Berlin. She was a distant relative of and shared the same surname as the

35

father of psychoanalysis, Sigmund Freud. My father, unlike my mother, came from a very religious and traditional family. His grandfather was the chief Rabbi of Budapest and our family had a strict Jewish up-bringing.

As a child, I was relatively happy. Obviously I had upsetting periods, especially when my parents were divorced, although from about the age of eight I knew they were not getting along well and there were times when my father was not at home. After they were divorced I was sent to a kibbutz and then later my mother remarried a pianist called Ladislas Gero, a widower. He had also escaped from Hungary and had formed a caberet dance team in Nicosia with his first wife. Later he took us all to Cyprus where my mother and he bought a small hotel catering to showbusiness artistes who were booked for acts.

My natural father was in the Israeli army and I visited him frequently, so I certainly did not feel deprived of paternal love. The only other thing worth mentioning is the fact that, despite being born in the so-called post war period, I was very aware of armed conflict throughout my growing years. Both in Israel, where I also had to serve time in the army, and in Cyprus where there was fighting between the Turks, Greeks, and the British. I give you this brief background of my history to help you understand my own PSI make-up. Case histories are always useful to study and you should do this continually when attempting to assess others. It can be very advantageous to you to build up a picture of the background influences affecting the thinking and minds of people with whom you will be associated in business or who will play an important role in your life.

I began using my powers positively in Cyprus. My stepfather had locked up a bike which was to be my Bar Mitzvah present. Like most impatient young boys, I could not wait to start cycling so I willed a combination lock immobilising it to open, which, after several attempts, it did. I also began making greater use of my mental telepathy, especially at exam time when I was able to read the answers other boys had given. Eventually my stepfather died and my mother and I returned to Tel Aviv where I was trained as a paratrooper in the Israeli army and was slightly injured in the Six Day War in 1967. I was then offered a job in a children's camp where I met Shipi Shtrang, one of the children I had to supervise. I ran into Shipi again later on because he lived next door to my father and we re-established our friendship. I am now married to Hanna, Shipi's sister, who gave me two wonderful children, Daniel and Natalie. It was Shipi who suggested I should demonstrate my powers in public and my first performance was at his school.

Mind over matter

In my lifelong career as a psychic I have flown to most countries in the world and have at times been concerned about my safety in the air. One particular incident in which I was not involved nevertheless captured my interest and attention because of the spectacular survival of the jumbo jet and its passengers while they were flying above Indonesia in 1982.

The British Airways jet called the City of Edinburgh was piloted by Captain Eric Moody. Eric is a matter-of-fact man who is happily married and lives in Camberley, Surrey, a beautiful suburb thirty miles from London. He gets easily agitated and impatient if little things go wrong but is totally cool and collected at times of grave crisis. At such moments, he has the doggedness of the British bulldog; he will not let go. There are two hundred and forty-seven grateful witnesses who would swear to that. They are the survivors of what could have been a tragic disaster when all four engines of Captain Moody's jumbo stopped working after his jet flew through a cloud of volcanic ash near Java.

For thirteen minutes, Eric and his crew tried in vain to restart the jumbo's engines. Can you imagine being in a jumbo gliding to earth with absolutely no power? How would you have felt after the jet had fallen more than seven kilometers and smoke had filled the cabin? I believe two things saved the aeroplane. The crew were positive, and Captain Moody's inner strength took on supernatural proportions, even if he did not realise it or admit to it himself. Gently and memorably he conveyed his incredible calmness to the passengers: 'This is your Captain speaking. We have a small problem. All four engines have stopped. We are doing our damnedest to get them going again. I trust you are not in too much distress.'

He would not give up. He and the crew were finally – and just in the nick of time – able to restart the engines at a low level. The passengers had been convinced they were going to die. But they did not panic. They prayed in unison. There was so much psychic energy within the aircraft that I belive PSI-FORCE was as much responsible for their salvation as the redeeming qualities of the Boeing 747 and its superb pilot. Curiously, one of the passengers had a vision of three figures working on the outside of the falling aircraft, mending the engines. Other passengers spoke afterwards about 'mystic feelings.' Their survival was described as a miracle. In psychic terms, it was an excellent and happy example of mind over matter.

No matter what I have done with my psychic powers in the past, I can never forget nor cease to admire the psychic forces in others, especially as in the jet airliner case I have outlined where so many lives were at stake. To me, it somehow pales my own achievements while at the same time giving positive proof that PSI power is there for anyone to use and that it can be used to benefit others.

While I may not consider my powers to be extraordinary, there are a number of reputed scientists who have thought otherwise after testing me for PSI. I think it is worthwhile knowing their views, if only to give you extra confidence in the existence of PSI- FORCE

Professor John Hasted, head of the Experimental Physics department at Birkbeck College, University of London, made a scientific study of aspects of psychic phenomena in the 1970s. He then published a book called *The Metal Benders* in 1981 (Routledge & Kegan Paul), and said of metal-bending: 'The essential phenomenon is this: a very few people appear to be able to deform and fracture pieces of metal, and occasionally other materials, just by stroking them between their thumb and fingers, or even without actually touching them.

'At first the household cutlery becomes deformed, no one knows how; perhaps a spoon or fork is seen to bend on its own. Usually the phenomena are first noticed after a television appearance by Uri Geller, the best known, first and "strongest" of all metal- benders . . . It is apparent that metal-bending should be classed as a psychic phenomenon, to be grouped together with such things as water-divining, telepathy, faith-healing, mediumship.'

Professor Hasted personally supervised various tests on me and reported on them. One involved bending two keys while he watched me closely. He reports: 'Geller was quite happy with the keys, and at once took one in each hand, holding it lightly between the forefinger and thumb; I did not take my eyes off them once, not even for a moment. I can affirm that I did not see Geller's other fingers touch the keys (except at pick-up) and that he did not move them more than about an inch from the table surface; they were in my field of vision the whole time. Nothing happened for about forty seconds, and then Geller put the keys flat on the table about two inches apart and stroked them gently, one with each forefinger. All the time Geller was talking, but I never took my eyes off the two keys and I am certain they never left the table for a surreptitious bend to be performed. After one more minute's stroking, the end of each key started to bend slightly upwards, one (the one stroked by his right forefinger) distinctly more than the other. The angles were eleven degrees and eight degrees, as measured afterwards.'

Professor Hasted also draws the attention of his readers to the fact that the famous psychologist Carl Jung 'had organised spiritualistic seances in his youth, and in one of these a breadknife in a drawer inexplicably snapped into four parts, with a sound like a pistol shot. The four pieces of the knife are still in the possession of the Jung family.' He also says he had personally experienced psychokinesis or teleportation. 'I have had to live with poltergeist phenomena on several occasions, and the experiences are not easily forgotten. I have kept notebook records of nearly a hundred "movements" of objects which I witnessed. I have records of many more reported to me by other observers of English cases.' He then describes how he observed an object being transported in my presence. 'Lynn (his wife) had started to tell Geller that she was entirely sceptical about metal- bending, and I was just entering the kitchen. I saw clearly a small object appear a few feet in the air and fall to the floor in front of the back door. It was about the size of the lid of our vacuum coffee pot, at first I thought that this was what it was, and that the pressure had blown it out. Geller turned round to face it, and we saw that what had appeared in the air and had fallen was a small Japanese marine ivory statuette of an old peasant. This had been in its normal place on the bookshelf in the lounge . . .' Professor Hasted's wife was shocked. But she was to receive an even bigger fright when a second object took flight. The professor wrote: 'Lynn's reaction was shock; she also believed it to be an inexplicable event and was frightened.

'We did not touch the statuette until it had been photographed. Lynn used her Polaroid camera, and obtained nothing but black pictures, which in itself could possibly have been a paranormal effect since she operated the camera perfectly well the same evening; but other explanations might also fit.

'While we were all standing around looking at the statuette, a second object appeared in the air and dropped. This time we all observed it, and it was clear to us all that it had not been thrown. It was the key of a Buhl clock which stands next to the statuette on the bookshelf in the lounge.' Levitation, another example of PSI-FORCE is also discussed by this scientist. He says: 'In British schools "levitation games" are sometimes played by children. A ritual is occasionally followed (e.g. running round and round a seated or lying child and chanting, "He is ill; he is dead" etc.); after the ritual, a number of children attempt to raise the body, each placing one or two fingers underneath it. The game starts with many children, who find the task easy, using only normal forces. The number is reduced one by one, and the continuing ease might suggest a paranormal contribution. The unexpected success has sometimes caused worried teachers to forbid the continuance of the game. I have found many children who insist that the body suddenly seems to lose weight,' wrote Professor Hasted.

I have met many other scientists who have tested me and observed my psychic powers. Wernher von Braun, the famous NASA rocket scientist was convinced of my PSI-FORCE. He tested me by holding his wedding ring in the palm of his hand and without me touching it the ring bent into an oval shape. I also made his electronic calculator work after it had stopped functioning.

Two laser physicists, Dr Harold E. Puthoff and Russell Targ, from the Stanford Research Institute tested me in laboratory conditions over several weeks in 1972 and 1973. Their results have been published in a book called *The Geller Papers: Scientific Observations on the Paranormal Powers of Uri Geller* (Houghton Mifflin Company 1976). In the introduction to that book, those scientists are quoted for the 'startling statement' they made about me: 'As a result of Geller's success in this experimental period, we consider that he has demonstrated his paranormal perceptual ability in a convincing and unambiguous manner.' Why were they convinced? The reason was that I had been sitting in a room which had been visually, acoustically and electrically shut off from the outside world. The book describes how: 'In another room down the hall, one scientist opened a dictionary at random, selected a word, and drew a picture of what it suggested. Geller's task was to "see" telepathically, and draw on paper each target picture. When, for example, the word chosen was grape, the scientist drew a bunch of grapes. Minutes later, Geller said over a one-way intercom that he "saw . . . drops of water coming out of the picture," and he spoke of "purple circles." Finally, when he was quite sure he "had it," he drew a bunch of grapes. The target and Geller's rendition of it both contained exactly twenty-four grapes.' In August 1973 the two physicists wrote in their paper *The Record*, of how they tried to make the tests even more difficult by not doing the drawings themselves but letting a computer draw the pictures: 'In one test a computer drew a picture of a kite on the face of a cathode-ray tube (a device similar to a TV screen); Geller drew a kite. Next a picture of a church was drawn and stored in a computer's memory bank; Geller drew a picture vaguely resembling the target. In the third test a picture of a heart pierced by an arrow was drawn on the screen of the cathode-ray tube and then the device was turned off. Geller perceived it correctly. From a total of thirteen such perceptual experiments the SRI scientists concluded that the odds for Geller's success being due merely to chance were more than a million to one . . .'

In another experiment: 'An ordinary die was placed in a small steel box; the box was opened after Geller wrote down his impression of the uppermost face of the die. This is called a "double-blind" experiment because neither the subject nor the researchers know the number until the box is opened. The test was performed ten times, with Geller "passing" twice because he received no psychic impressions. But the eight times he did record a number, he was right every time. The odds: about a million to one. In another test, also under double-blind conditions, Geller located a hidden object placed in one of ten aluminium cans. He did this correctly twelve times in a row, with odds of over a trillion to one. He also mentally altered the reading of an electrical scale and disrupted the workings of a magnetometer, a device that generates an electric current from radioactive source.'

At about the same time I was also tested by scientists

from the Naval Surface Weapons Center in Silver Spring, Maryland. I bent a metal alloy wire made from nitinol. This wire springs back into its original shape when heated but after I had bent it, the wire refused to do this. The scientists came to the conclusion that I had used paranormal means to deform the wire. What particularly interested one of the institutions testing me was my apparent ability to interfere with computers. Scientists from the Lawrence Livermore Laboratory, one of the top physical research centres in America, watched me successfully stop two computer cards from working after I rubbed my fingers across them.

My way

I could relate many more experiments where I have been tried and tested and successfully puzzled even the most sceptical scientists with my powers. But that is the subject of other books. I have given you this background information in the hope that it will already partly explain some of my techniques and at the same time show you what *you* could do.

So how do I do it? Basically the method is much the same whenever I use my PSI-FORCE but even so, I will explain my methodology by taking you through various situations which could arise.

Telepathy: This involves the communication by extra sensory perception (ESP) of one mind with another mind or a telepathic source like a computer. One person sends a message to another person using only the mind.

First of all it would help if you trained yourself to think visually. The best way of doing this is to close your eyes and imagine you are looking at a television set in your mind. Draw an imaginary screen in your mind, ready to tune in to a picture of your making. Take your time, and as discussed earlier, do a few exercises to relax yourself. Relax your mind and your body and just concentrate on your mental television screen which at this point of time should be blank. Now turn on that imaginary TV. Actually imagine yourself pushing a button or turning a knob and let that screen flicker to life. Now start putting images on that screen. The face of someone close to you, the house or flat you live in, your favourite pet.

Now go back over some of the day's events as if they had been recorded on your personal video and play those images back to yourself. With practise, this becomes quite easy to set up and to 'replay' your own home movies on your mental TV screen.

The next part of the exercise may take a little time and effort. Imagine you are a receiving station. You are waiting for the video film to be transmitted to you although you do not yet know what is on that video. Imagine you are a few hours ahead of time and see what images you receive on your screen. Practise this constantly.

When you can virtually command the TV screen to appear in your mind at will, ask a friend to draw a simple picture on a piece of paper without showing you and see if you can draw the same picture. Try and make that image materialise on the TV screen in your mind. With practise it should do so. I am a stout believer that telepathy is within most people's ambit and that with enough practise, *you* can do it.

If your friend has not been able to project the picture, keep practising. Do not give up straight away. Ask your friend to trace over the picture he or she has drawn several times. Then, if all else fails, try another friend who has a more positive approach to PSI or telepathy. If you don't feel confident that you can be telepathic, just think of the number of times that you have come out with the same sentence as someone else in your company or the number of times you knew who was on the telephone as soon as you heard it ring. These are all indications of telepathy.

If you are able to successfully read minds, try sending messages to another receiver. Draw a picture on a piece of paper and ask your friend to replicate it. Be relaxed about it. If you find you are tense and irritable or under pressure while doing it, stop and try again later. You have to feel confident. Telepathy can also be practised with the following useful 'props.'

Cut out a series of numbers on cards. Take one of these card numbers and concentrate wholly on it. Put it into your mental TV screen and then see if your friend can correctly say what number it is. Try the same with a pack of cards and see if your friend can guess either the number, the colour, or the suit. Another series of images to send could be simple shapes like circles, triangles, squares, and crosses or choose simple capital cities or six famous people and see if you can send their facial images to your friend. Keep it easy at first and then you can progress to more difficult images and concepts.

When I receive information I can see a line appearing in my imaginary screen and it actually draws the image or letter from the right to the left. If the drawing stays in the screen for six seconds or more I know I am right.

Sceptics believe there MUST be some trick. Many times my brother-in-law Shipi is accused of being my plant, of sending me signals, even smoke signals. And there have been stories about transmitters secreted in my teeth, about 'hearing' pens draw, about peeping through my fingers, even seeing through envelopes with a powerful light. But the many scientists who tested my powers know this is absurd – whatever some magicians continue to claim about me. There are NO technical tricks. Otherwise I would have been found out countless times and exposed years ago.

Now here's a fun thought. Why not invite friends around for PSI parties? Metal bending was even written up in the prestigious *Washington Post*, and now metal bending parties are already very popular throughout the States, why not extend it to telepathy and other fun PSI skills. Why not begin a new craze!

How I start watches: Many people have been able to start watches moving again after seeing me on television. Somehow, I have given them the confidence to be able to do it themselves. I was quite happily shocked once to receive a telephone call from a scientist called Dr Thelma Moss who told me that she fixed broken watches in her classes just by letting some students see me on a video. It then dawned on me that my powers had stimulated the dormant powers in others. If someone brings me a broken watch I do the following things: first I wind it up, whether or not it is broken. I hold it in my hand, it does not matter whether it is the right or left hand, and then I talk to it. Yes! Talk to it. I also visualise it working. I tell it to 'mend' and to 'work.' I put all my mental concentration into making it tick. I tell myself – I virtually psych myself and let myself know that I can feel heat coming from my hand. 'Tick,' I command, 'tick!' and in most cases it begins to tick. Naturally some sceptics claim that if you shake or warm a watch, that will start it going. But what about the thousands returned from watchmakers that could not be fixed? Watchmakers say to me that they have given up on watches which I have started up again. You have to concentrate all your efforts on what you are doing. The same may apply to household objects which

47

no longer work. Televisions, hairdryers, even a car has been known to start working again using this method. Remember that a strong element of this is *believing* you can make the object work again.

Spoon bending: Here I switch from words like 'work' or 'mend' to the words: 'bend' or 'melt' and 'break.' I relax my other senses and then put all my concentration and energy into making that spoon obey my commands. I like to let that energy run through my body into my hand which then transfers it to the spoon although I have been able to bend metal without even touching it. But obviously it is much easier for me to transmit energy to the spoon by touching it. Sometimes it seems to change its molecular structure and the spoon becomes soft and bends or breaks. Of course, I am often debunked as having prepared the spoon beforehand. This is ridiculous. I would have been caught cheating many times over. Equally outrageous is the notion that I use chemicals on the end of my fingers to bend metal and cutlery. My fingers would have dropped off. And what, too, of those thousands of children and adults who have also experienced this phenomena? Are they and their witnesses inventing their stories?

Sprouting a seed: Seed sprouting is an act I perform as few times as possible because it actually scares me. It interferes with life. And, as yet, no sceptic or magician has been able to explain this. I make something grow, like radish seeds for example. I close my hand on them and *will* them to sprout. The phenomenon is fantastic and the bud usually sprouts. The process of time has been condensed. Usually it could take up to a week to happen naturally but with me it happens in a few moments. I really concentrate deeply and focus my mind on exactly what I want to happen. I can really visualise seeing that seed growing on my imaginary TV screen. It's fantastic when the bud comes out!

Deflecting a compass: I can feel the PSI-FORCE energy coming out of my eyes and my forehead and so I bring my forehead close to the compass which should be lying untouched on the table in front of you. Sceptics think I have hidden magnets in my teeth, hair, or neck, or even swallowed one, but of course I do not. It is proof to me that we have so much energy in the mind because I can always make the compass needle deflect when I put all my PSI effort into moving the needle.

Dowsing: This is a very touchy subject because multi-national companies have spent hundreds of thousands of dollars paying me to dowse for precious minerals. However, although the directors have every faith in my powers, they are wary about making public my findings in case they are criticised by unbelieving members of the public who are their shareholders and who might consider them cranks. Even so, I have gone on record already by naming mining companies, with their permission, who have successfully sought and received my services. Dowsing in its most familiar form, employs a divining rod, originally a Y-shaped twig which is held by the diviner until it begins bending, sometimes with a violent action, in the direction of water or whatever the person dowsing has sought to find. I do not use a twig but dowse with my hands, usually with both hands fully outstretched until the palms of both my hands begin to feel the vibrations of what I am searching for. I get a feeling in my hands as though two magnets were drawing the palms of my hands towards my goal. It certainly does not matter if I am looking for gold, oil, diamonds, or water, although I personally have an affinity for metals.

Professional dowsing has happened to me in the following way. A company contacts me and I ask it to send maps of the area they want searched. I examine these maps very carefully, sometimes spending hours or days, thinking about it and feeling the area with my palms outstreched above the map. If I get a feeling that something is there I will continue with my research, if not, I suggest to the company that I am not the person for this job. If I feel there is something there I ask for geological reports and more information on the general area. Then I will fly over the area and ask the pilot to circle when I feel sure I have the right spot. It is not a fast process and I feel a great responsibility to the company concerned because of the millions it can cost them to invest in drilling and research. Consider this: if my detractors were able to duplicate these successful mining explorations, they too would be multi-millionaires!

You could start off in a smaller way. Draw a layout of your room and get your friend to hide an object. Then see if you can find that object, first by placing your palms above the drawing and then by walking around the room with outstretched hands until you feel the vibrations or force in your hands telling you that you are in the vicinity of the object you are seeking.

I successfully performed such an exercise on the David Frost breakfast TV show in Britain towards the end of 1986 when a valuable ring was hidden in one of fifteen identical matchboxes. They were all together on a dish. I moved the palm of my hand carefully above each matchbox 'feeling' for the right sensation. That was not easy. Eventually I was sure I had narrowed it to just two of the matchboxes. The ring would be in one of these two, I said. I was certain. And it was. Millions of viewers, and the studio personnel were amazed. I had scored. You should try the same thing with say five or six matchboxes and progress from there.

Premonitions: If you have a premonition, especially one where by acting on it you feel you can avoid a disaster, I suggest you do so. I have heard so many stories where people were going to get on aeroplanes or jump into a motorcar before a crash and did *not* listen to their premonitions. Well, that is wrong. You must listen to them if they are that positive. There may never be another chance otherwise.

Use your premonition, which is a type of pre-cognition – prediction of the future – in business and social dealings as well although this will be more fully dealt with in a later chapter, when I will also tell you about the premonitions scientists and famous stars have experienced.

Gambling: I feel this exercise can be an abuse of powers and will investigate aspects of it more thoroughly in a later chapter on numerology and cosmic forces. I once predicted correctly the numbers of a dice eight times out of ten, 'passing' twice when I received no impression. This test was conducted at the Stanford Research Institute under laboratory controlled conditions. I have won vast amounts of money at casinos, though not without a certain amount of suffering afterwards. But I have also lost money in casinos and I do not recommend gambling for high stakes although it can be fun to have small bets with friends.

PSI-power and communication

A friend of mine who recently visited the Indian sub-continent had a most frustrating time getting a taxi to take him to the beach at Bombay. Every time he asked a cab driver for a lift the response was the same: the cab driver would shake his head in a strange undulating fashion from left to right, which my friend interpreted as an emphatic 'No.' In each case, the cab he flagged down had been empty, and other passengers would step into the car or motorised rickshaw after he had walked away in disgust, contemplating what his personal failings might be or wondering whether he had just caught a strange disease which only Bombay taxi drivers could identify. It was only after several 'rejections' that he began to wake up to what was really happening. The truth of the matter was that, far from rejecting him, each cab driver had expressed a willingness to accept the fare using the locally recognised body language of shaking the head to indicate acceptance. My friend's frustration came about as a result of his failure to communicate properly. He did not understand that the Bombay driver's gesture in shaking his head from left to right meant 'Yes!' and nodding the head meant 'No.'

Communication is one of the most important aspects of our lives. The better we can communicate the more successful we are going to be. We spend most of the time we are awake communicating with others and yet so few of us take the trouble of perfecting techniques which could revolutionise our lives. Understanding body language is a very important part of the technique of communication, as is 'reading people' and being on the same 'wavelength' as others. That is where PSI power can be such a useful and vital force. It can be used to help in understanding the real message people are trying to put across to you, or alternatively, conceal from you. Timing is another essential ingredient of communication. Choosing the right moment to say something can mean the difference between success and failure in achieving a goal.

How good do you think your communication skills are? I would like you to do the following test and ask you to be absolutely honest with the answers. Afterwards, add up your scores as outlined below. I will then show you how to use PSI-FORCE combined with practical know how to become a more effective communicator.

Testing your communication skills: Answer either 'Yes' or 'Not Sure' or 'No.'

1. Are you good at interpreting body language?
2. Are you sensitive to the needs of others?
3. Do you notice immediately if someone is getting bored with the conversation?
4. Are you a good listener?
5. In general, are you good at handling people?
6. Can you always tell if someone is offended by one of your jokes?
7. Are you good at 'summing up' other people?
8. Can you tell immediately if someone takes a liking to you?
9. Are you good at predicting who will become friends with one another?

10. Can you always tell when someone has something on their mind?
11. Are you good at sensing how far to push someone?
12. Do people often come to you with their troubles?
13. Do you think you can tell when someone is lying?
14. Can you sense immediately if a friend is in a bad mood?
15. Can you predict when someone is about to burst into tears?

Scoring: As in the previous test, score 2 points for each 'Yes' answer, 1 point for 'Not sure' and 0 points for 'No.'

If you have scored 14 points or more, then you are 'in tune' with others and can read the relevant signs. Body language is to you just another means of communication. You are the type of person who is easy to get along with and who other people turn to in times of trouble. If your score is 24 or more you are well on the way to achieving thought transference!

A score of 13 or less indicates that you are not used to communicating with others. You have been introverted and taken up with your own life to such a degree that you are somewhat oblivious to the needs of others. You must learn to observe other people and be sensitive to their needs. This is a skill you can easily accomplish with practice and a little help from your close friends.

While it obviously helps to master a language, I must also point out that you do not need to be an honours graduate to be an effective communicator. My first language was Hebrew but that did not stop me from being invited as one of the keynote speakers at the annual international Young Presidents Organisation seminars in New York. I shared the platform with distinguished people like Henry Kissinger, Alexander Haig, and a former President of the United States, Mr Gerald Ford. Also at the YPO were powerful giants of business and industry, people like James Robinson, the chairman of American Express, and the legendary oil king, Texan T. Boone Pickens (beside him the Ewings of Dallas are mere paupers!).

An essential ingredient of being a good communicator is to be an even better listener. If *you* do all the talking, you will be unable to properly assess and understand the person with whom you wish to communicate. Let the other person do the talking, initially at least. That gives you the psychological advantage of responding to a situation of which you now have some knowledge and control. Listen to what that person has to say and as you do so, study the speaker's physical actions. Without realising it, most of us subconsciously take account of body language but I suggest you really make a point of becoming aware of this aspect of an individual's personality. It will help you so much more if you pay particular attention to all the physical manifestations accompanying speech. And remember that while that person is talking, you can be responding favourably without saying a word by using your own body language which we will discuss later in this chapter.

Throughout my years as a public figure, I have had to entertain both friendly and hostile inquisitors. Curiously, I have found that 'like species' of humans are not altogether different from the animal species in behaviour patterns. Take Boxer dogs as an example. They are powerfully built animals which, if exercised properly, display splendid physical shape. But to anyone who does not understand these dogs, their facial features can project an image of viciousness and ferocity. Nevertheless, a common trait is that they are as soft and cuddly and friendly as a child's teddy bear, although there are always exceptions. People who understand the breed will have no hesitation in approaching the dog as if it were their own and it will undoubtedly respond in a way they expect – most probably by licking them all over the face! But someone who does not understand the breed will probably elicit a completely different response, depending on the approach.

In a similar fashion, we have taught ourselves to react to different 'types' of humans, even though we may not be aware that we have. Every one of us probably has a library of 'faces' which we have categorised without thinking about. As an exercise, try and write down 'types' you know and make a note of your feelings towards them. Your responses will obviously be flavoured according to your personal experiences in the past. For instance if you have had a bad experience with a tall man who is balding, wears pince-nez, and has a moustache, there's a good chance that you will be wary of his look-alike.

You might categorise men with balding heads and beards as being of a certain psychological make-up that you either like or dislike. Or you may like women who have red hair and freckles and not be at all interested in blondes. Whatever categories you describe, write down what you like or dislike about them and then try and analyse why you feel the way you do. Very importantly, you must also write down the psychic vibrations you get from each personality type. If by doing this, you can overcome basic prejudices, you will be helping yourself greatly because vibes are a two-way thing. The other person is just as likely to 'receive' feelings of hostility from you.

I always look for 'clues' when talking to people. I tend also to get a general preconceived impression of the individual by placing the person according to my idea of personality type. I then try and assess that individual by his or her mannerisms (body language) and from what is said. Instinct is very important but it must be developed with the PSI factor which consists of your overall impressions and feelings towards that person. I switch on my PSI button and pause and study the person with my inner mind. It is like hitting that person with a surge of psychic energy and waiting for the feedback. The feedback should usually tell you a lot about the person and whether or not to trust him or her. You have to trust your own intuition about the feedback you get. If you have any uneasy feelings about the person then you must allow your intuition to rule. Take notice of warning lights. So often I hear people saying: 'If only I had followed my instinct.' Listen to your suspicions, but at the same time make a conscious effort not to communicate your own negative feelings to that person.

Body language

Like any other form of communication, this is a two way thing. You must learn to be aware of the other person's physical actions while at the same time controlling your own. This is where you need a lot of PSI-FORCE assistance. Psych yourself *not* to give away your own feelings to the other party if you don't want them to see you in a certain light. Remember that thought transference is a powerful medium and what you are thinking may be easily 'read' by the other person if your body language manifests your deepest thoughts. Go to the mirror again and practise facial contortions. See how well you can adopt different expressions. That does not mean that you have to show an inscrutable face; that in itself can be a giveaway. Concentrate on the following:

Eyes: Try different expressions when in front of the mirror. See if you can look angry, happy, sad, interested, amazed, calm, and in love. Eye contact is one of the most powerful physical means of communication. Did you know that when lovers gaze into each other's eyes, their pupils can dilate? Looking someone else boldly in the eye gives the impression of confidence and honesty. Someone who casts his eyes down or sideways and is afraid to look into the other person's eyes will give a bad impression, which could be taken for dishonesty, inferiority, or weakness. Establishing good eye contact without appearing to be over intimate is essential. Watch out too for tell-tale signs of narrowing around the eyes, or darting movements. A lot of people find this emotion difficult to control.

Mouth: Take careful note of other people's mouth movements. The way they purse their lips, and particularly the way they smile. A smile can readily be recognised if it is false or nervous or even angry. Primates sometimes bare their teeth in a 'smile' when they are about to bite. Stand in front of the mirror and articulate your mouth to see how many different expressions and meanings you can come up with. Ask your partner to do the same and see if you can read each other.

Nose: Apart from the obvious feelings of disgust which can be so powerfully projected with the nose, many people use it as a focal point of other expressions. Tapping the nose with a finger can mean the person is thinking about what you are saying without being convinced, or they can be getting impatient with you, or just plain suspicious. Another manifestation is steepling the fingers of both hands in pyramid fashion and bringing them up to the face or nose. The chin is another favourite spot for stroking in times of uncertainty or when in thought. Watch the person's brow. That too can be a giveaway. Watch carefully for the slightest twitch or furrow. The head itself is another indicator. Watch the way it tilts or nods. Have you ever studied the way Britain's Prime Minister, Mrs Thatcher, tilts her head in an expression of interest, almost like a bird listening to different sounds?

Hands: These are very important. The way you hold a wife or girlfriend, husband or boyfriend, can tell a lot about the way you feel for her. Handshakes are important and should vary with your judgment of the other person. If you are going to shake the hand of a Canadian lumberjack, put all you've got into it. If it is someone of a more delicate nature then you should adapt the handshake accordingly. If the person you are communicating with is fidgeting with his or her hands don't let that put you off. Alternatively, if you think it is your fault and you are boring them, stop talking and provoke them to take up the conversation. Nervous people tend to clasp their hands frequently and if you are of such disposition you might do well to take a leaf out of the British royal family's book and firmly hold your hands together behind your back if you are walking or calmly sit with your fingers intertwined. Prince Charles is particularly expressive with his hands. He has learned to use them to overcome a basic shyness and nervousness when appearing in public. Avoid fast or agitated movements with your hands because the way you control your hands forms a very important impression on other people. As long as you are aware of this and practise acceptable and confident gestures with your hands, you will soon get into the habit of communicating successfully with your body.

Prince Charles, more than any other member of the royal family, uses body language to its limit. I think it has a lot to do with his interest in PSI and his efforts to project his inner feelings and thoughts to other people. Like an actor, he has a range of expressions for different situations. He is an excellent listener. He shows deep interest and concern by using his face and hands. He tilts his head, furrows his brow, fingers his ear lobes, looks intently at the person with whom he is communicating and shows a riveting interest in whatever he is being shown. Similarly when he speaks, he demonstrates an intense caring which he is eager to project to the other party.

Princess Di on the other hand is not so accomplished at body language as the Prince. She has courted the 'Shy-Di' look which has almost become a trademark in itself. Rather than display her emotions she has tended to 'hide' behind a cultivated look although she will change as the years progress and already she is showing signs of strength and independence. Like Charles she will begin to use PSI-FORCE and project her inner strength.

The Queen and Prince Philip are total professionals at body language, especially the Queen. She is able to control her feelings superbly yet, if she wants to make her displeasure known, has only to contort her face slightly for maximum effect. Although the Queen is a very private person, she also relies on PSI power to read people and situations and it is by using this ability that she is able to project her own feelings so capably. The body language message from her is clear. She has an imperial and inscrutable look. The public want to see this. Her Majesty must be seen to be apart from the masses, while caring for them and loving them as her subjects.

Compare this to President Reagan. His message to the public is: 'I am a homely, happy and a loving person.' He does not mind exposing his inner weaknesses while at the same time insisting on an outward strength. The message has been successful. Americans like outward-going people. They want to feel he can be trusted; at heart he is one of them.

Marilyn Monroe talked to the world with her mouth and eyes. While men might have worshipped her body, it was the facial message that attracted them initially. She invited the world to her side. Humphrey Bogart was another great master of facial body language. A few subtle movements of the eyebrows and lips and slow baring of his teeth sent fans wild. Less subtle but equally effective was Elvis Presley. His body language was that of a raw savage which appealed to millions of women. He used all of his body to bring across his message.

I believe the message of PSI has also come to the Soviet Union and is especially being adopted by the new regime. At its head, of course, is Gorbachov, the Russian leader whose own body language and PSI projection is masterful. He has charmed and angered the West at the same time and showed he can play their game at being Mr Nice Guy just as effectively as a Western leader.

All the people mentioned above may have used and adopted facial expressions observed in those less famous. But what they have, or did have, is a kind of aura which in PSI terms is sometimes described as a form of radiation around one's body signifying a state of spiritual development. Clearly it is an indefinable element which can best be explained as a highly developed sense of PSI which is effectively projected and then received by the public, who in turn hold those people in awe and great esteem.

PSI-sensitivity

Being sensitive to the needs of others requires inner thought and PSI transference. People often convey messages which they do not intend or mean. They can be shielding their innermost secrets by feeding false information but at the same time they might desperately want to tell you their fears. You can work on this by drawing them out further than they intended to go, by being sympathetic to their story even though you know it is not true. Watch for the giveaway body language which contradicts their speech. Think about what they are saying and concentrate your PSI power on their true thoughts. Never break into their thought pattern if they are speaking. Most people will eventually commit themselves verbally and reveal the truth without you having to do anything other than be a good and sympathetic listener.

Another factor that you must take into account is cultural and physical differences with the persons with whom you are communicating. Get on their wavelength! If someone is older or younger than you, their experiences will be different from yours. Try and understand their viewpoint in the light of their experience and not your own. They might have a different educational background from yours. This does not in itself mean your conversation need be limited. Steer the conversation onto a mutual level of understanding. You will also find communication problems with people of different nationalities and occupations and religion but these are minor problems which skill, patience and understanding can easily overcome. If you have language difficulties, try body language and psych yourself to get in tune with the other person.

If you tend to be a person who does most of the talking, watch the other person for signs of boredom. If they cross their legs, fiddle with their hands, look away, fidget, then you are not captivating them with your words and you should stop and steer the conversation their way. There is nothing worse than boring your friends or people who you want to impress.

You must combine all the qualities mentioned above if you want to make a good impression on someone. In addition, it is important to dress for the occasion. If the person you want to impress is of a conservative nature, you should dress accordingly. People tend to judge others by their own standards and you should always do your homework thoroughly before meeting the other party. Always be polite, give a firm handshake and be a good listener. Do not interrupt and do not look impatient. Tailor yourself to what the other person says. If the other person is interested in boats then talk about them, even if the subject is not interesting to you. Do not be pushy and try to reflect an inside warm feeling towards the other party. Send him or her warm suggestions. Say to yourself: 'I like you. I think you are a good person.' The positive feeling you project is bound to be picked up and felt by the other party.

The art of being a good listener is to physically show

the other person that you are interested in what is being said. Body language is the main cue for this. A nod of the head when agreeing, a tilt when expressing great interest in a particular point, perhaps a show of puzzlement, the occasional verbal reassurance. All these are indicators to the other person that you are a sympathetic and good listener and your movements will reinforce and reassure the person with whom you are communicating.

Choosing the right moment to communicate is as important as the communication itself. I was standing in a New York subway once when I noticed a father and son engaged in what appeared to be a violent argument. The pair were oblivious to the public gallery who were intrigued by their verbal confrontation. As their exchange became more heated I suddenly noticed a friendly but dangerously insensitive man approach them announcing that he was from out of town and could they direct him to Greenwich Village. Father and son stopped dead in their tracks in disbelief. I thought they would turn on the man but fortunately the father had a sense of humour. He said to the interloper: 'If you don't mind, we are in the middle of a fight, go and ask someone else for directions.' That might seem to you to be a rather extreme example of an insensitive person choosing the worst possible moment in which to strike up conversation but I can assure you it is absolutely true.

PSI projection can also be used in the following way: as well as projecting your own good feelings — or bad — to the other person, try and swap roles with the other party. In other words imagine you are the other person. Use your PSI power to imagine how that person would react to *you*. Then when the actual communication takes place, you can respond in the way you imagine that person would either have expected or liked you to have responded.

Always be aware of the importance of clothes and personal appearance. The type of clothes a person wears can have a great bearing on that person's behaviour. Although I have not been to any of these parties myself, I am told by some of my English friends that occasionally they are invited to a 'vicars and tarts' party which is a quaint English way of loosening inhibitions. The thinking behind it being that the ladies will act like 'tarts' if they dress like them. Young boys will feel 'tougher' wearing leather jackets and boots but their behaviour can change dramatically if they are suddenly made to wear a suit and tie.

A useful exercise you can do is to write down points about a person's clothes and habits and see how much you can learn about that person without even speaking to them. Remember too, that environment is a great influence on the way another person behaves. Someone on holiday can be quite a different person away from the stress of business and home. Equally, meeting somebody for the first time on an aeroplane can leave you with quite a different impression from the one you might otherwise form of that person, if you met in different circumstances.

Extracting information from people is not always an easy task. Most of us only listen to what we want to hear. By that I mean that many of us want to confirm our own prejudices or be aware of our anxieties. What you must learn to do is to think and relax before you engage in an important conversation and then set yourself apart from your normal beliefs and attitudes and allow the other person to explain his or hers to you without interruption. To do this will take practice and patience but it will be very rewarding if you are successful.

Leaders in our society are those to whom others will listen and respect. They will, almost by definition, be effective communicators and generally speaking have good judgment regarding other people. Whether or not they admit to it, they will have a highly developed sense of PSI.

Communication traps: Rising to the bait: don't fall for this common trap and allow anger to rule your emotions and detract from the quality of communication. Psych yourself to resist and overcome hurtful comments. Make sure you control your body language in moments of crisis.

Trick questions meant to throw you off guard: say nothing rather than something you might later wish you had not said. Project your innermost thoughts in a positive manner and keep calm.

Gossip: engaging in idle gossip can be quite fun but be aware that you too could be the object of gossip and it is advisable to be a listener rather than a participant if the gossip gets particularly vicious. You might falsely be accused of being the perpetrator.

Emotional blackmail: children and lovers are masters of the art of emotional blackmail and you must use every bit of PSI power you can muster to understand what is behind it. Don't act rashly but concentrate your innermost thoughts on swinging the conversation away from this dangerous path.

Psychological dominance: don't be afraid that just because the person you are communicating with is in a much higher position than you or is far better qualified than you are, that he or she is necessarily your superior. Be polite and courteous but treat him or her as an equal. Don't look down or away or be reticent or subservient or nervous when entering the room or place where the communication is to be held. Instead show confidence by standing upright and establishing and maintaining a proper level of eye to eye communication. Television interviewers are masters at putting down people who have never before appeared on television. Just by organising disadvantageous seating arrangements and camera angles they can make the untrained person look like an inept beginner. Have your wits about you all the time and if in doubt, cancel the interview or make it happen on your own terms by laying down ground rules before you begin.

The over-friendly interviewer: don't let yourself give too many personal secrets away to the over-friendly interviewer who pretends to be your instant buddy. He or she may be fishing for information while giving nothing away about themselves.

Voice and speech: The words you use and the way you speak will tell a lot about you to the trained observer. Even the volume of your voice will give an insight into your character. If you speak in a loud voice you will be associated with being a dominant and aggressive personality striving for success. But there may also be the hint of superficiality while a soft voice will be associated with timidity and a non-assertiveness. Perhaps the answer is to modulate your voice as the situation demands.

Good, clear, and precise pronunciation is the hallmark of a well formed character with few inhibitions and a positive outlook on life whereas the reverse is true of people who are bad at getting their words across clearly. Practise what you want to say to give the best possible impression.

Fast talkers tend to be impulsive and sometimes emotional but if you are confident in what you say, it will tell the other person that you are a positive, if somewhat aggressive personality whereas slow talkers can give the impression of being logical and cold.

In later chapters, I will teach you how to out-psych your boss and bank manager but for now, do all the mirror tests I have recommended and read this chapter on communication several times and then combine it with your PSI power. Afterwards try your new approach on friends and colleagues and note the difference it makes!

The PSI factor in positive thinking

Having reached this chapter, you will by now be aware of the power that you possess and which, if you have not already put to good use, you soon will. I hope too that you are convinced that your inner power is a *positive* force and that to be effective it must always remain positive. PSI-FORCE exists in your mind but it will only be released with positive impulses. Believe in *yourself*. Believe in your ability. Believe in your power. Expel negative thoughts and feelings. Banish them from your mind! Negative thoughts and worries are like a cancer. They will spread through your mind and body until they destroy you. Positive thoughts will overcome them easily providing you allow them to. I am giving you this opportunity to write your own prescription and overcome the condition of depression, unhappiness and emotional insecurity. Be your own healer. Prescribe for yourself the most beneficial medicine in the world. POSITIVE THOUGHT. POSITIVE POWER. Write it out now. It's free! Psych yourself to think only in positive terms. Wake up in the morning and be grateful that you are alive to face the adventure of another day. Tell yourself that PSI power is going to make the day a good one for you. Believe that positive things will happen. Don't let the negatives get you down. Fight them with an army of positives.

Positive thinking leads to positive action which in turn can bring fulfillment and happiness in work and social activities. A positive attitude can turn business or school failure into success, despair into happiness, and if you have been ill, it can certainly help to make you healthy.

Before I show you how most effectively to use the PSI positive factor, let's see how much of a positive thinker you are. Try the following test answering each question with either: 'Yes' or 'Not sure' or 'No.'

The Positive Thought Quiz:

1. Do you think of yourself as younger than you really are?
2. Do you have self-confidence in abundance?
3. Do you tend to do well under pressure?
4. Can classical music inspire you?
5. Are you opposed to the idea of retirement?
6. Do you have the opposite of an inferiority complex?
7. Do you sometimes think anything is possible?
8. Are there many occasions when you are fired by great enthusiasm?
9. Are you adept at turning bad luck into something good?
10. Are you very persistent once you start on a project?
11. Do other people consider you the energetic type?
12. Do you very rarely have gloomy thoughts?
13. Are you excited by new hobbies?
14. Do you often feel 'on top of the world'?
15. Do you crave the excitement of a new challenge?

Scoring: Give yourself 2 points for each 'Yes' answer, 1 point for 'Not sure' and 0 points for 'No.' Now add up your total score. If you scored 17 or more points the likelihood is that you are a positive thinker. That is a good start because with an attitude like yours, you are more likely than others to succeed in life and to make the most out of opportunities offered to you. But you must remember that many successes in life are attributed not so much to genius as to plain hard work and positive thinking! If you are a borderline case or fall well below 17 points, then you must re-assess your whole life and your image. A score of less than 17 does not mean you will be disadvantaged, but you have still to learn to overcome negative feelings. If you do you will be much happier with your lot. And happiness often brings greater success. You can become a positive thinker by building up confidence in yourself and by making a conscious effort to improve and cast out negative feelings. One of the best ways of doing this is to find out what you are really good at. It might be sport, music, writing, sewing. It might be computers, painting, quizzes, cooking or dancing. No matter what it is, work on it until you are so much in demand that other people come to you for help, advice and instruction with your particular skill – as people did in earlier days when they turned to the local scribe, for example, when they needed a letter to be written.

This will bring you respect from others and even more importantly, it will help you to increase your *own* self-respect. Then, use PSI power to influence others in the way I have shown you throughout this book. Let's face it, what is there about doctors or dentists that most people admire so much? The answer is knowledge. They have a specialised knowledge and skill which gives them extra status in the public's eye because theirs is considered to be a vital profession. But what you might not realise is that many doctors and dentists are very down-to-earth people who consider the skills of others to be no less important than their own. I have many medical practitioners among my friends and they will show as much respect for the skill of a mechanic who would mend their broken car as he would have for them for mending a broken limb. So, whatever your calling in life, do not underrate your own worth but concentrate on improving the skill you possess.

Even if you are a naturally positive person, which I believe I am, you must still learn to concentrate all your positive energies into making things happen. When I was wounded in the Six Day War, I was told by doctors that I would have incredible pain in my arm during the mending process and while receiving physiotherapy to straighten it. Although I was unable to move the wounded arm more than ten degrees, I insisted on playing basketball and continuing a normal life. I refused to acknowledge the pain and concentrated my mind on limiting the pain. Negative thoughts were telling me to feel sorry for myself and to stay in hospital. My positive thoughts told me I would forget the pain and continue as normal. Within a very short time I began using the arm again and within eight months I could almost straighten it without any pain at all. I do exactly the same with headaches and other maladies that afflict us all from time to time, but more of that later.

Positive thinking helped me win a promotion and rise from tea boy to a junior executive in an export company I worked for in Israel. I was young and confident and thought I had the world at my feet but after starting the job I felt quite insignificant and lost a lot of my self-respect. My self-importance vanished when instead of sitting at a smart desk, as I had imagined before starting work, I was made to be a lowly tea boy running errands. That's where PSI power came in. I was not going to let myself be or feel inferior for very long, so whenever the boss was in the room I would fix him with a concentrated stare – when he wasn't looking – and give him the following mental message: 'You have to keep Uri and give him a promotion. Make him a junior executive. Upgrade his position. He's worth every cent.'

It was not long after that that he called me into the office and said: 'Uri, I have a surprise for you. I'm giving you more responsibility and money. You're going to be a junior executive!' Well, it might have been a surprise for him, but it wasn't for me. I had convinced myself that through my positive PSI-FORCE energy I was going to get that promotion.

I also believe that positive thinking saved me from freezing to death on Japan's highest mountain on the island of Honshu. Mount Fuji is an extinct and beautiful volcano which rises to over 12,000 feet. I own a holiday cottage near the base of this mountain in central Japan and late one afternoon I had the urge to jog to the summit. Being keen on physical fitness, a fifteen to twenty-five kilometer jog in a day is no problem. But mountains can be very cold and about two kilometers from the summit I began to suffer from the effects of hypothermia. I was only wearing a singlet and shorts and became quite shivery.

I became concerned. If I continued to the top my condition would worsen and my strength was rapidly leaving me with the extremely low temperatures of the late afternoon. Hanna, my wife, would not know where I was because I usually ran around Lake Yamanakako and by now it was too far and too late to turn back.

I knew, however, that there was a car park and restaurant at the top of the mountain and that cars would soon be making their way off the montain. I could hitch a lift with one of them. With that I made for the road, but despite my sorry look and digital pleadings, nobody stopped. Japanese people do not like stopping for hitch-hikers so I still had to find a solution to my problem.

I needed to get off the mountain and I would not give up with the cars. Someone would have to take me. Positive thought: that was what was required. I would have to stop a car using PSI power and the positive thought factor. I figured that the next car that came around the bend would be my taxi and confidently told it to stop. 'Stop, stop, stop,' I repeated in my mind. But nothing happened. If only I could speak Japanese. I then began to visualise the following scene. I saw myself in the centre of the road with a red car bearing down on me. The car would have to stop and I would be invited inside. I imagined a young couple in their twenties driving the car.

And then it happened. Within five minutes a red Toyota car screeched to a halt in the middle of the road. I was standing at the roadside but the car stopped as if it was avoiding an obstacle. I went over to the car and two young people just looked at me in surprise. I indicated, using my hands, that I would like a lift with them down the mountain. They were thrilled when I told them who I was because they had seen me on Japanese television. My positive thinking had stopped their car and saved me from freezing.

I had used similar mental energy some time earlier when I stopped an escalator and a mountain chairlift in Germany. Thinking of Germany reminds me of another example of positive thought, but with a little spice added to it. I hasten to mention that at the time of this story, I was a footloose and fancy-free bachelor and could therefore be excused from my positive but naughty thoughts.

I was in Munich at the time and as part of my daily exercise I would run through the town's English Garden where lots of extremely pretty girls sunbathed semi-nude in summer. Invariably, they would be lying face down to preserve their modesty; and like every hot-blooded bachelor I was keen to see the bits they were hiding. To do so, I told myself, required positive thought power and I imagined a situation where two of the girls were being buzzed by a giant hornet. I concentrated my energies on these two girls and relayed a telepathic message: 'Watch out! watch out! A hornet is coming. Get up quickly!' With that both girls jumped up looking terrified but on seeing me they giggled with embarrassment while fumbling to hide what I had set out to see.

The positive principle

Through mind control you must learn to separate your problems and put them in different compartments in your brain. Otherwise they will blur other and more important issues and not allow you to operate at maximum efficiency. If a problem gets you down, your judgment could be vitally affected in crucial issues so you must learn to look at your problems from afar. Treat them as if they are not your worries but somebody else's. The secret is to shut out and block niggling fears and worries and concentrate on more important matters. There are several ways of doing this and through trial and error you can find which one suits you best.

I suggest that you clear your mind entirely, shut your eyes, and meditate. This can be done anywhere. In an office, at your desk, anywhere at all where you can find a few moments to yourself. You can then imagine a series of 'in' and 'out' trays or 'pending' trays or even little boxes in your mind. Put your work in one of these trays, your leisure in another, personal relationships in yet another and your negative thoughts in the last box. Say to youself: 'I will shut that box and now concentrate on another box.' Do whichever activity you want to concentrate on. You can create any number of boxes to suit the occasion. If you want a box for difficult decisions, create one and then slam down the lid and lock it up until you want to examine the problem again. Having learned to do this, say to yourself that you will not let the problem box interfere with you, that you have too many important decisions and other positive matters to contend with. By doing this you may never need to open the problem box at all. A lot of difficulties are solved with the passage of time, and through 'sleeping' on them when your subconscious mind takes over and solves the problem without wasting your conscious energies.

Never allow problems to keep you awake at night. When you are tired or sleepy it is the worst time for solving problems and you must learn to shut the door on these detrimental influences as otherwise your capacity to cope will be further impaired the next day through lack of sleep.

If I have difficulty in sleeping at night, here's what I do. The minute I hit bed I visualise a large master switch and see myself walking across to it and turning it off. That also switches off all my problems and I have a pleasant sleep. If the problem is one that will not go away, like illness, then I suggest you lessen its seriousness by making comparisons with those less fortunate than yourself. Look to the positive side, no matter what. A friend of mine almost despaired after being thrown from a show jumper into a tree. He broke many bones in his body which his doctors said would take a considerable time to heal. I cheered him up by pointing out how lucky he was. He would make a full recovery. That's the positive side. The accident was so serious that he could easily have been paralysed for life and confined to a wheelchair, and at worst, he could have broken his neck and died.

Whenever you want to use your PSI-FORCE to maximum effect, you must try and relax your body completely. Look on it as a brief period of battery charging before the positive energy begins to flow again. I will say more about this when we come to the subject of health but it is important to mention here that the stronger your health and the fitter you are, the better you will be able to use your PSI energy to deal with problems as they arise. I have even found it possible to meditate on a crowded London tube train, so don't think it is essential to wait until you get home and into the privacy of your room before you can start this very important process.

Worries

There are some worries we all have that will never be solved or go away, yet we still express concern about them. Why? Because we are all insecure to some extent and we need reassurance and comfort. I am not suggesting you become totally self-reliant but I would certainly recommend that you try and solve those worries by yourself. Get help, certainly, but don't idly discuss worries just for the sake of it.

That is being negative. It may sound cynical, but why worry when it doesn't matter? So much energy and time is wasted on useless worries. Worry can be like a disease and your body must resist it.

Psi power can help you solve your problems with positive energy. Although you are in a position to shut off a problem or worry, you may still have to solve it. Don't run away from problems. Dissect and analyse them in a positive way. Find out the main ingredients of the problem. Consider and identify what it is you are actually trying to achieve to get over it. Think through carefully the different ways there are of tackling it. Write them down. Don't ever be frightened to ask the professionals for help. If you have a money problem, bank managers are much more sympathetic if you discuss the issue with them instead of ignoring their letters and hoping they will go away. See them personally, communicate with them and give them a good impression of yourself. All they will really be interested in is whether you are a reliable person who will pay his debt. Tell them what they want to hear and then do what you have promised. In future you will be able to negotiate loans over the telephone because you will have established a favourable 'track record.'

Relationships can be a constant source of worry and upset and negative feelings, but much of that is caused by low self-esteem. Don't be a slave to other people's emotions. Psych yourself to be strong and not worry about temporary breakdowns. Many people play psychological games of dominance over others. You must learn to read the signs when those games are being played. Listen to what is being said. If statements are made as a deliberate untruth, their purpose may be to upset you and make you vulnerable. Don't fall for it. Let your PSI power make you independent and impervious to hurtful suggestions and malicious gossip. People will accept you for what you are today, not for what someone told them you were yesterday.

Most highly successful people could not care less for things said about them behind their back. They are confident enough in their self-esteem and position not to let it bother them. It is a sign of insecurity to allow yourself to be plagued with negative feelings arising from petty jealousies and gossip. And the people who matter and who like and respect you won't usually allow their feelings to be influenced unduly. Tell yourself not to worry. Say to yourself that you will not be affected by negative feelings and comments and then forget they were ever made. You will be surprised how quickly they will disappear.

Rationalise your failures

I don't think there is anyone alive today who at some stage or another has not had to cope with failure. Positive thinking can turn that failure into success. Learn to treat failure not as a personal loss but as an important lesson for the future. Today's failure could make a millionaire of you tomorrow. Let me give you a shining exmple of that. One of the world's best-selling authors whose books are read by millions and have been turned into popular TV series – *Kane and Abel* and *The Prodigal Daughter*, were just two of his successful ones – was not so long ago an unhappy bankrupt. He had placed all his own money, and a lot more which he borrowed, into a Canadian company that went bust. With debts of nearly a million dollars he could have slipped away quietly and stayed a bankrupt for the rest of his life.

Instead, Jeffrey Archer picked himself up and wrote a book about his experiences. It was called *Not a Penny More Not a Penny Less* and became the forerunner to making him a millionaire author. He was able to pay back all his debts and now owns a beautiful penthouse overlooking the Thames in London as well as a country manor near Cambridge. No matter how adverse the circumstances, his positive thought power conquered his past failure and made him a greater success than he had been before his bankruptcy.

The author Frederick Forsyth was once a hard-up freelance reporter. No one was very interested in his impassioned representation of the Biafran case during his reporting of the Nigerian Civil War. He returned to Britain and wrote a series of novels like *The Day of the Jackal* which made him a multi-million dollar fortune.

Another success story is that of the English publisher Robert Maxwell, who I have met at a society party in London. Bob has an air of total confidence and is notable for the aura surrounding him. Yet in the early seventies, a government report said he was unfit to lead a public company. His was a classic rags to great riches story. He was born in Eastern Europe of humble Czech parents and fled from the Nazis who had murdered members of his family. Today, this unstoppable workaholic tycoon – who is chauffeured in a lilac Rolls Royce – is the head of one of the largest newspaper empires in Britain, a successful book publishing company, satellite television interests and is regularly featured in financial newspapers for his company takeover bids and further acquisitions. Instead of being considered a failure, he is today a captain of industry.

A victim of circumstances

All of us are, to some degree, victims of circumstance. Our view of life and our actions are the product of the influences surrounding our upbringing and our experiences. Psi growth can make you aware of how those circumstances have affected you, and once you understand the reasons, positive thought power can help you either grow out of your product self or, if you are happy as you are, maintain your status quo. If you are unhappy and cannot come out of yourself, then you are in danger of being a slave to those circumstances which have adversely affected you.

Take the role of a housewife. That is a very important role to my mind, because traditionally the matriarchal figure is one of strength who holds together a family and runs the house. Because of pressures in our society, many mothers feel threatened with this traditional role – of which in the past they were proud, holding themselves in considerable self-esteem. In today's world, women have changed their views considerably and many mothers feel that a career is as important, if not more, than the traditional role. In fact some traditional role mothers feel their self-respect is threatened by *not* going out to work. The purpose of this book is not to argue the merits of either side but to reassure both modern and traditional mothers that what they choose to do and are happiest doing is the *right* decision and they should take no notice at all of those critical of them for their choice of direction. You must do as you wish and not feel a loss of self-respect simply because others are doing the opposite. Staying at home with the children does not mean you will stop pursuing interests and skills.

They are just as available at home as in the office. In some ways it is even better than 'vegetating' in a boring office job. Similarly, a woman who chooses a career in preference to staying at home can still give her children and family all the love and care they need without suffocating them.

The important principle to be constantly aware of is to psych yourself against unnecessary and cruel comments which are inevitably made. Feel proud of your role. Be confident and happy about it. Tell yourself that what you are doing is the right thing and nobody can change that position. Be positive. If you are happy with your lot, nobody can take that happiness away.

Some people tend to 'give up' and accept their role as the victim. You hear them say: 'I'm always the one who is blamed,' or 'I'm always choosing the wrong partner' or 'It doesn't happen to anybody else . . .' Why is it that some people make the same mistake time after time? The prime reason is that they have not given their minds time to think about their failure and turn it into a success. Psi meditation and positive thinking could change all this. Use the techniques in communication which you have learned to 'interview' the person with whom you want a relationship. Think back on your past experiences and send out positive vibes to the other person.

I can never stress enough that, no matter what your background, you should never feel 'inferior' to other people and therewith accept certain situations that could with positive PSI power be avoided or overcome. Your positive PSI will tell you that you are as good as the next man, whether he employs you or teaches you.

I will never forget the story which was told to me

by an American friend whose cousin, a pretty young Philadelphian girl, married an English mill worker during the Second World War. It was a perfect example of negative acceptance, although I hasten to add that it nevertheless had a happy ending.

The Englishman had been called up to serve in the British Navy and his ship sailed to the East Coast of America where he met the girl. They became sweethearts and married before his ship sailed back to Britain. After the war, the British government flew his wife to Wigan in Lancashire where they began a happily married life and had two children. Before the war, some of the Lancashire mills had been putting men off work and this mill worker, in common with others, had no security in his job. Matters did not improve after the war either, although the young couple were very content. Like all young women, she wanted desperately to show her children to her mother back home in Philadelphia and was given a one-way fare by her mother for this purpose.

She returned to America but could not afford to come back to her husband because he was out of work again. Sadly, the pair accepted their fate and although they loved one another they agreed to divorce because they could not get back together. Both remarried and each had two further children by their new spouses. She kept in touch with her first husband by sending Christmas cards. Thirty years on, she wrote to say her husband had died leaving her a wealthy widow. By an amazing coincidence, his second wife had also just died and she suggested they meet again. This time she flew over with her own money and they married for a second time round! While this is a beautiful and true story, I could never have accepted the fact that my loved one would be away from me for ever. I would want to swim the ocean rather than 'accepting my fate.' Yet in their own way, both these people were positive about their future but not secure enough about their position in life. What would you have done? How would you have used PSI-FORCE to bring you together?

Your physical self

So much importance is placed on physical appearance that there is a natural tendency to feel second-rate if you do not look like a Miss World or have the physical stature of Tarzan. But just look at the way positive thinkers have conquered their shortcomings. Many cruel comments have been passed about short men but think how sucessful lots of short men have been. Have they strived harder to overcome what they considered to be a personal 'failing'? Would anyone have dared look down on Napoleon, on Charlie Chaplin, on Aristotle Onassis?

The deposed Shah of Iran, who was also a short man, had a most effective way of teaching others to respect his 'height.' Whenever the country's newspapers printed photographs of him with the Queen or dignitaries, he was inevitably represented as being taller than the others. I inquired of one of his ministers how this was so and was quite taken aback to be given the following explanation: 'Ah,' said the ruler's confidant, 'the Shah invites the editors of the newspaper to a few days "protective custody and instruction" if they slip up and make him look shorter in the published photographs.'

Once you have accomplished something, you are not remembered so much for your physical shell as for what you represent. Your physical appearance becomes a visual identification factor only and you are recognised for your inner self. And everyone has the capacity of making their inner self appear beautiful, attractive, and interesting.

Regrets

Don't waste time regretting the past. Rationalise your mistakes. Just as you did with failures, treat them as another learning process and get on with your life. There is absolutely no point in negative thoughts about what could have been if you had only done so and so. Shut your eyes and relax your mind. Tell yourself that what has happened is no longer of any consequence. Put it out of your mind. Close the lid on regrets. Tell yourself that whatever happened was going to happen anyway and that you could not avoid the inevitable. At least you now have the chance to start again. Think about today, not yesterday.

Prayer can be a very helpful aid in defeating negative thoughts and eliminating unhappiness. It can be used as a form of meditation, a PSI process where negative thoughts are dispelled and where you can come to terms with what has happened before and recharge your batteries for the present. People with a strong faith and belief have a very positive side to their character which can assist them greatly with troubles in life.

A complex fantasy

Everybody talks about the complexity of life. But what about the complexes themselves? We are riddled with them. Our comic books are based on them. Take Superman: he is the same physical person as Clark Kent, reporter. But does Lois fancy Clark? No. She is in love with the image of super-strength. She also shows a very poor understanding of PSI because with proper communication she would soon tell that Clark has the same qualities as Superman. That great humourist Woody Allen is always missing out on beautiful girls on the screen. To some extent he probably does in real life too, but because he has become famous by screening his complexes, I am sure there are countless women who would be more than willing to share those complexes with him.

If through PSI you overcome pessimism in small matters, you will then be able to handle larger disappointments. Count the number of times, if you can, when you have been a nervous wreck about deciding what to wear to a party. Was it worth the worry? If you were concerned about being over-dressed then you were probably the centre of attraction because you were 'different.' Or alternatively, nobody cared anyway. What about the times you have been worried about arriving late for a dinner or an appointment only to find that the hostess wasn't ready anyway or the other person was late? I don't advocate being late, but once you are, there is precious little you can do about it, so why worry. Make the most of it with positive thoughts. Instead of worrying about it, make up a good excuse. The positive person is the one who has fallen into the ditch but always comes up 'smelling of roses.'

From now on refuse to accept that you will be the last person to be served in a shop. Make your presence felt through PSI. Don't be afraid to complain about a restaurant meal if it is bad. Do it politely but communicate effectively. Don't ask meekly if it is all right for you to walk into a room. Do so proudly. Don't put yourself down. Stop being a victim and an underdog. You are just as important as anybody else. Think positively. Think PSI!

Love and the PSI-force

Psi-power coupled with good practical advice can make *you* a better and more attentive lover. It can help you choose the right partner and establish better relationships. It can also help you deal with loved ones and relatives at home and teach you to avoid the pitfalls of emotional entanglement. While doing this it will also teach you more things about *yourself* as well as your partner, which should bring about a better understanding for future relationships.

Love is one of the most powerful and positive forces in the world. From the moment a baby is born and its umbilical cord is severed, it receives a fresh injection of the life-giving force that is popularly called 'mother love.' Without it, a baby can suffer serious consequences. One of Britain's foremost baby experts, Dr Hugh Jolly, who, before his death in 1986, was Physician in charge of Paediatrics at the world famous Charing Cross Hospital, recognised the 'instant telepathy' between a mother and her child. Having spent a lifetime studying the behaviour of mothers and babies, he was convinced of the invisible PSI bonding that took place in that charged moment of birth. Babies who were fortunate enough to have this love, accompanied by cuddling and tender physical touch, thrived, unlike their unfortunate and pitiable counterparts who were deprived of a mother's love.

Dr Jolly, who was known as the Dr Spock of

Britain, said that this telepathic bonding was a gift of nature and would continue through the child's growth, although as its intelligence increased and it gained verbal skills and learned body language, a new form of communication techniques would gradually replace the PSI communication which nature had bestowed on the child.

The fascinating thing to remember is that the original power to communicate love by means of telepathy was never permanently lost. Certainly the baby will stop using PSI just as its mother did when she was little, but then look how quickly the mother regained it when giving birth to her own child! Now why, when it is possible to use this powerful force, do we let it lie dormant for so long?

The essential ingredient of love is communication. Even if two people do not speak to each other there can still be communication in the form of body language and physical attraction. The more successful you are as a communicator the more likely you are to succeed in the love stakes. Learning to interpret the signs, learning to 'read' people and understand 'feelings' is all part of the PSI-factor of love.

You need see no greater proof of the power of love than in nature itself. I once had the sad experience of seeing a graceful bird, a swan, pine for a lost mate until it gave up hope of ever seeing its partner again and tragically died of a broken heart. Domestic animals have been known to pine to death for their owners and most pet lovers can tell stories about the amazing animal telepathy they have encountered.

Recently, an actor friend of mine who appeared in the classic film *Out of Africa* with Robert Redford and Meryl Streep, had an important show to do which took him away from his home for about a year. He was very fond of his black cat with which he had an amazing PSI bond, and rather than board the cat, he asked a friend to mind it. After he had been away a few months, he returned to his home to collect some clothes and was there only a couple of hours when his cat, which was living some miles away during his absence, unexpectedly appeared on his doorstep wanting to be let in. Until that time, the cat had been quite content to remain with his friend. The remarkable Welsh sheepdogs whose affection for their masters is legendary, are known to develop an uncanny telepathy in their bid to please. I have seen dog trials where communication between man and beast is almost entirely telepathic.

Sexual attraction

Sexual attraction, if we are honest, is probably one of the first 'moves' in the game of love. You must learn to accept that fact whether you are beautiful, attractive, or plain. Only then can you begin to work on improving your chances of success.

Obviously, character and personality play a very large role but that comes into it later because most of us are primarily captivated by the best display in the shop window.

As with all rules, there are exceptions, the main one being that of the person with 'star status.' There, looks can be quite irrelevant and the 'image' is often the thing that first attracts, rather than the physical features. Those people who are fortunate enough to have both are either very lucky or very tired!

I am often asked about my own experience in these matters and am prepared to forgo my modesty for the sake of instruction. As a young man I did not have much trouble attracting women because through good fortune of birth I happened to have what are considered reasonable looks and I was tall. Even though I was not well-known then, I could use my PSI power to attract women. I knew how to engage their interest by concentrating my energies and establishing strong eye contact. Once we began talking I found most of them were captivated by PSI, especially if I demonstrated some of my powers. When I became publicly well-known the response of the opposite sex was overwhelming. Wherever I went women were falling over themselves to meet me and their fascination was never-ending.

That kind of adoration is quite a difficult thing for a young man to cope with and I must confess that I happily made love to many women. With all that experience it became very easy to tell just by looking into a woman's eyes whether or not she would be willing to go to bed with me.

On my first trip to Europe from Israel, I had an affair with the wife of a German industrialist. She was as rich as she was beautiful. She wanted to spoil me like I had never been spoiled before. I had sports cars at my disposal, butlers serving my every need, heated swimming-pools and luxury cottages in the beautiful countryside just awaiting my call. It was a far cry from home where I had lived in a cramped flat and driven a motor scooter. After our affair had finished, countless other ladies were ready to step into her shoes. Women had a great fascination for my powers. They wondered what it would be like to sleep with Uri Geller. I can't imagine what they had in mind for while I was quite happy to bend metals and demonstrate my telepathic powers, I was not prepared to experiment with the human anatomy! But back to serious matters, I had learned that PSI-FORCE had given me a very powerful weapon which to many women was an instant aphrodisiac — fame and fortune.

Let me give a note of warning here: relationships like those I have described above can be very empty. For a young man sowing his wild oats, a fling can be fun in the short term but like most normal people I wanted something more out of a relationship. I needed a permanent, stable, and loving relationship which I have since found with Hanna, my wife.

I realise too that most of the women I knew as a carefree bachelor were more interested in the 'image' and 'fantasy' than they were in me as a person. Again, I do not feel there is anything wrong with 'fantasising' on a temporary basis but it is certainly not the thing on which you can properly build a lasting life together.

Nevertheless, most of us fantasise about prospective partners. To people we find attractive, we tend to attribute all sorts of qualities we admire. Many women are attracted to tall, lean and handsome men. They see qualities in these ideal physical types which they associate with strength and leadership and intelligence. In reality of course, it may be nothing like this but our views are heavily influenced by traditional 'images' of physical types.

The converse of this is true as well. If we have a romantic intellectual image of someone, then we will give them a body to fit. Take the English poet John Keats as an example. He was nearly as much loved in America as he was in Britain and many of his romantic poems were inspired in London's Hampstead, where he once lived.

Anyone who has wandered around Hampstead Heath on a lazy summer's day cannot help but visualise the poet writing an ode under one of the centuries-old trees in this beautiful and historic park. What physical image would we give this tragic figure who died a miserable death from TB? A traditional one that people have described to me is of a tall, sensitive young man with a handsome, lean face. They imagine him wearing a cloak as he strode purposefully across the heath. The image is further compounded with the view that he would enchant friends and admirers with language so poetic that it could attract the nightingale. The correct image of the man is far different: Keats was short, stout and abrasive to the point of sometimes being quite objectionable. An image his admiring followers a hundred and fifty years later do not wish to recognise.

I am not recommending that we stop fantasising about our heroes or heroines, or the people we love or think we would like to love. All I am suggesting is that we *do* recognise that there may be a fantasy involved, so that when the reality becomes all too apparent it does not bring us back to earth with a hurtful jolt. No one likes to be bitterly disappointed.

The cosmos of love

When we meet a partner we always look for indicators of love and compatibility. Astronomical calculations predicting personal characteristics in your partner – astrology – are common. Were you born under the same star sign? Is your star sign compatible with that of your partner? Do the same numbers influence your love life? Whether or not we apply these signs in a serious way is questionable. If we love the person enough, we will somehow explain or rationalise an unfavourable star sign and hope the relationship survives. Nevertheless, we continue to look for reinforcement. For my part, I can recommend no better reinforcement than the application of PSI and good practical sense. It has worked for me and I am sure it will work for you.

Relationships

Learn to evaluate your own relationships through PSI meditation and self-analysis. Here's how you do it. Relax your body and clear your mind of all thoughts. Try and keep this state of relaxation for some minutes and then draw the word 'RELATIONSHIP' on a screen in your mind. Now visualise the people or person with whom you are having a relationship. Start with the most important relationship first and ask yourself relevant questions which can also include any doubts you might have. Here are some suggestions.

1. What am I looking for in this relationship? Be honest with yourself. Do you want this relationship to be long-term or short-term? Is it a relationship of convenience or one of true love or merely companionship? Your expectations from any relationship will vary according to your particular classification. How much of yourself do you want to give in this relationship? Are you prepared to accept the other person for what he or she is? It is much easier to put up with other people's bad habits if you know the relationship will not go on for very long. Now try and visualise yourself with the other person. Project your mind and imagine how you and the other person would be seen by a third party. Would they see you as a compatible and happy couple?

2. Is the relationship a happy one? Think back on all your previous relationships and determine whether the present one is better or just the same. If you are not happy, ask yourself why and see if you can think of ways of improving it or whether it would be better to end it and start afresh with someone new.
3. Am I on the same wavelength as my partner? Ask your partner to try some of the tests in this book and see how closely the answers resemble yours. Does your partner or friend like doing the same things as you? Are your interests the same or similar? Are your jobs and your aims compatible? If they are not then your relationship may suffer or, alternatively, it may explain things if you are not getting on so well. Make sure your partner tries the tests involving mental telepathy.
4. How would I see myself if I were in my partner's or friend's shoes? Psych yourself to change roles. You become your partner and imagine how *you* are seen in the relationship. What faults do you see? What improvements could you make?
5. Is my 'image' of my partner a real one? Are you fantasising about the qualities of your partner? Do you really know him or her well enough? Does the image portray the real self?
6. What is your ideal of a partner or friend? Ask yourself what your ideal partner would look like. Would he or she be tall, dark, blonde, or short? What other physical qualities would you look for in an ideal partner? What interests would you like your partner to have? What standard of education? Then look back

and examine your past relationships and see how close you have got to your ideal. Ask yourself whether you think *you* would make the ideal partner or whether you consider you have shortcomings, and if so, what are they?

7. Are your astrological signs compatible? Does your partner share the same birth sign as you? Are your stars compatible? If you have looked at other signs like numbers or tarot cards, is there a conflict?

8. How well do you communicate with your partner? What is the level of your communication? Do you find it easy or is it difficult? Are you sometimes able to communicate without talking and know what the other wants? If you can, then there is a very strong PSI link and the chances are yours will be a successful relationship.

9. Do you harbour a resentment within your relationship? Is there something he or she has done which you have either not fully discussed or perhaps you have refused to discuss and are holding back? Perhaps your partner has an annoying habit and although you try your best to ignore it, it still aggravates you. If that is the case your relationship will suffer and with negatives of this nature it is best to air them before resentment overcomes your positive feelings and breaks up the relationship.

10. Would you prefer to end the relationship but do not have the heart to tell your partner? This is where you must really think carefully and be totally honest with yourself. Many relationships are continued through habit and not through personal choice. Some people

find it easier to coast along in a relationship than to face the truth that it has floundered. Learn to read the signs. Do you telephone that person as much as you used to? Do you see them as often? Do you think about them? Concentrate your mind on these questions. Meditate on your relationship and look for the PSI factors which will tell you how *you* really feel about the other person. If other questions or doubts occur to you, write them down and ask yourself or your partner. Be honest in your relationship. If you cannot improve it then there is no point in continuing something which has ceased to be a pleasure.

How PSI can make you a better lover

PSI power can make you a better lover. I will teach you, through a series of fun PSI games, how to laugh and love with your partner through the medium of PSI. These new games are guaranteed to bring you closer together as well as teach you to understand each other better and to get on the same wavelength.

Before each game, do the relaxing exercises I have outlined. Help each other to relax. Either sit comfortably together in a sofa or your bed, and close your eyes and see if you can concentrate on the same television screen in your minds. You might find the signals between you are so strong that you will receive each other's telepathic signals before you have a chance to start the games.

Psi love games   Colours: Start with a simple game of colours. Cut out squares of paper and write down the names of, say, six colours. Red to symbolise passion and sensuality; White for purity; Purple for health and peace; Blue for intelligence and happiness; Gold for ambition; and Yellow for uncertainty. You can use these cards in several different ways. One of you can hold a coloured card in your hand and telepathically convey the mood you feel to your partner. He or she must then read your mind. Alternatively, you can lay all the cards face down without seeing in which order the colours appear and then each of you tries to choose the colour RED or any other colour you care to nominate. Hold out little rewards for your partner if he or she reads all six cards correctly. Alternatively, you can reward each other every time your partner reads your mind. I will leave the reward you give each other to your own imagination.

Messages of Love: Write down six different coded messages which you and your lover use as an intimate expression of love. It might be the name of a certain part of your anatomy, it can be a pet name you use for each other, or suggestions either of you makes. One of you selects a card and then attempts to transfer the message to the other partner. If the identification is positive the correct suggestion could form part of the reward!

Psi-tease: This is a great game for people who are married or living together and can add spice and excitement to their love life. Tease your wife or partner with this PSI game which you can play in your bedroom. Your partner is blindfolded and made to sit in a chair facing away from you. Tell your partner to relax completely and make sure he or she cannot see you. Now if you are wearing the blindfold try and imagine the TV screen in your mind and picture the room with your partner in it. The partner not wearing the blindfold can now take the initiative and begin to tease. Take off an item of clothing and ask your partner what it is you have removed. If he or she guesses correctly, carry on with the game. The next thing you might want to do is to adopt a yoga position on the floor or sit in the bed. See if your partner can picture this. Each time he or she guesses correctly you can reinforce the PSI game with a kiss. You can eventually remove most of your clothes – or put on different ones and see if your partner can visualise what you are wearing or not wearing. It might be suspenders and stockings that you have put on, or it might be something that will satisfy another fantasy your lover has about you. Whatever it is, make sure that you surprise your partner and reward him or her adequately if the answer given is correct.

Another intimate love game involves thinking of six different things your partner really likes. It could be a back massage, running your fingers through his or her hair, or just holding hands. Challenge your partner to do one of those things at a time and see if he or she has correctly received your intimate desires.

Love signals

Positive thinking and PSI power will help you attract a partner if you plan your approach carefully. Understanding communication and body language is of enormous importance in making the right impression. Most first encounters with the opposite sex result in empty chat but an interested awareness in the physical qualities of the other party. If you feel you have physical shortcomings, then make the most of nice clothes and immaculate grooming. That will more than make up for physical inadequacies. Try and meet the person you are interested in on several occasions. The more contact people have with others the more interested they become in one another. Learn to read the signals the other party is giving you. If the other person is a man, try and find out if he is more interested in you as a sex symbol or as a person. Look at the way he views other women. Stereotypes are easily recognised. The man who makes a play for women with big breasts is normally an extrovert and sporty type. A 'bottoms' man is likely to be tidy and neat, an accountant perhaps, and a 'leg' man will be loud, sociable and an extrovert.

'Read' what he is saying to you. Work out if it is a chat line or whether he is genuine. If you show no interest, see how quickly he moves to another lady and tries the same line.

If you are a man you must observe the signals of the opposite sex just as carefully. Is she gesturing and posturing with her lips and body? Is she giving you eye contact or does she look away and act bored when you speak? Her body language will let you know whether or not she is interested in you. If she is warm and accepting and looks into your eyes while smiling, you may be impressing her with your presence. If she touches your hand, brushes her hair and makes other 'preening' gestures while talking to you there is a good chance she will want to speak to you again.

When you want to show a woman that what you want is something more than conversation, try and psych her with love. Look into her eyes and tell her in your mind that you want to kiss her and make tender love to her. If you say that, all your thoughts will reach her. But do it gently, let the unspoken words gently float into her mind, as though you are singing your love or reciting a beautiful poem. Don't frighten her. You will know immediately if she responds. This is the power of telepathy in love. It is a harmonious connection and it is the way a lot of people fall in love at 'first sight.' There is a joining of the minds. By psyching yourself mentally the whole body reacts and if the feelings are right you can cause a chemical explosion which will bring you both together. Often this is described as a chemistry of the minds. In fact it is PSI power triggering a chain reaction of physical impulses.

But I must stress that your physical self plays an equally important part. You must be clean and presentable and it helps if you can attract the other person with nice clothes or good make-up and coiffured hair, especially in the initial stages where looks still count. Afterwards, as I have already said, you must concentrate on personality and effective communication. That is the discovery stage where each partner wants to impress the other while at the same time learning all about the other party. Think of all the PSI positives at this stage. Both men and women love to be reassured that they are liked and are seen as being attractive. Small gifts like flowers, chocolates or a short personal note or letter are a very effective way of conveying this feeling.

Psi guide to loving: There is no reason for lovers to rush that very special act that brings them into spiritual and physical harmony. Love is not just a physical act. To reach a better understanding and a more fulfilling sex life you need to be mentally alert to each other's needs and desires. Before making love I suggest you first go through a process of PSI meditation. It does not take long. Do it while you are cuddling. Clear your mind and just concentrate on your physical presence. After relaxing, think about your role you will be playing as a lover. Try and imagine the beautiful things you can do to one another. If you like, talk about it. Project yourselves on a different astral level. Imagine you are both riding the universe. Transport yourselves away from earth, metaphysically speaking of course. Do this successfully and your love life will never be the same again!

How to beat the system

'Mr Geller,' requested my bank manager in an unexpected telephone call, 'I wonder if you would be kind enough to drop into my office for a chat. Say three o'clock tomorrow?' Why did he want to see me? I couldn't figure it out because I had just requested a bank overdraft and was told that approval would only be a formality. Had I inadvertently drawn more money than was agreed? I was quite puzzled and a little worried as to why I should be requested to appear in person at the bank. I had only recently opened the account after my first big television appearance in England and although at that time I was not rich, I had sufficient funds owing to me to cover loans and overdraft facilities.

At the appointed hour I was ushered into the manager's office, a large room with wood panelling and soft leather chairs in the financial heart of London. The manager, conservatively dressed in a pin-striped suit, bespectacled, and a little overweight, eyed me with some uncertainty. I did not say a word but looked at him firmly in the eye which seemed to unsettle him slightly. 'I'd like to talk to you about finances and your overdraft,' he began, 'but first let me explain a few things. You're in a position where you meet beautiful women, you appear on television, and you are hosted around the world. We bank managers lead a very sober existence. We sit here all day enclosed by four wooden walls, running our eyes over client accounts. Rarely do we get the chance to have such an exciting life as you must lead. For the sake of some of my staff downstairs who have to work in the vaults, would you mind bending a few spoons?'

'But what about my overdraft?' I inquired. 'Oh, don't worry about that,' he responded. 'Now, how about some tricks, eh? I've told the girls downstairs that you were coming and said if you were prepared to show . . . ' It did not require a genius to realise what the cunning manager was up to. He only wanted me there to raise his own standing among his staff, and in particular with the pretty secretaries working for him. Well, if I was going to be used like this I might as well get my pound of flesh I thought. 'I'll be happy to do it,' I replied, 'but let's get the business over and done with first. I know I asked your bank for an agreed overdraft facility but actually that won't be enough. I'll need double.' Just at this point, the secretaries walked in for my 'spoon bending performance' and before the manager could use their arrival as an excuse to fob me off, I insisted we finish discussing my finances.

There was nothing he could do. Not wishing to appear mean or hesitant in front of his staff, he immediately agreed to my demands and we got on with the social aspects of my bank visit, which, after all, was why he brought me there in the first place.

I tell you this true story because it is important to understand that everyone is human, even bankers. And like everyone else they have their weaknesses. The manager had used his position to get me into the bank. He was totally in control of the situation until the secretaries walked into his room. At that point he was sitting at his large leather-topped desk 'holding court' with someone he thought would elevate his own status. Had I not asked for anything he would have tried to continue in his dominant role.

My demand threw him temporarily off balance and the only way for him to have retrieved his position in front of the secretaries was to appear generous and accede to my wishes. I had in fact turned the tables on him. He could not possibly have refused my request without a massive loss of face. Both the timing and the demand were perfect.

I often wonder why so many people I speak to are afraid of their bank managers. Let me tell you, unless they are bullying aggressive types – and even then sometimes – they are probably more scared of you than you are of them! Treat the bank manager as your equal. That does not imply that you show him disrespect. You can still be courteous and pleasant without demeaning yourself. Learn to play a clever game using PSI and body language to get your own way. If you want a loan, don't go cap in hand to the bank manager. Don't feel that you are a second-rate citizen just because you need money. Most successful people have huge overdrafts. Go in there with the attitude that you are doing *him* a favour. By giving you an overdraft the bank is making money which helps to keep it in business and employ staff. You are doing everybody a favour by borrowing. *You* are the customer and the bank should be nice to *you*.

Like anybody else in life, the bank is likely to turn nasty or be mean to you when it feels threatened. It feels this threat when it considers, rightly or wrongly, that you are not going to pay back the money you owe. There are ways of overcoming misunderstandings and these can be summed up with one word: 'COMMUNICATION.' Keep in touch with your bank manager. Tell him what's happening. Don't wait for that offensive letter. Take the initiative and write first. Unless you tell him about your problems he won't know what's happening and may think the worst.

Reinforce the bank manager's trust in you by fulfilling your promises. If you have told him you will put money in by a certain date, then do so, even if you have to borrow from elsewhere. If you cannot borrow the money, then write to him and explain why it will be impossible to deposit the funds as you promised. It doesn't take a great effort to do this but I can assure you it will really pay dividends! The bank manager will respect *you* as a person who is in control of the situation and as his estimation goes up, so will his willingness to allow you increased loans and overdrafts.

Invite your bank manager to lunch and charm him with your positive PSI personality. Talk to him about investments and banking, a subject he should know a lot about and therefore feel confident in discussing. This will also make him feel important. Find out about his other interests like sport or photography and discuss his favourite topics. Psych yourself to send out positive vibes. Use telepathy to tell him you like him and urge him to like you. Invite him to call you by your first name and he should respond accordingly. Once you establish a friendly relationship he will do all in his power to accommodate your requests. The benefits a good lunch with your bank manager will bring you, will by far outweigh the cost of the meal. Next time you are in the bank and he passes by, make sure you greet him by his first name in front of his staff. They will give you better service in future and think twice before sending you unfriendly letters of demand.

The short cut route to success

Have you ever driven down a twin lane highway and found one of the lanes traffic logged while the other is almost empty of cars, even though there is no compulsory turn off at the end? I have on many occasions and never cease to marvel at the patience of the British public. I put this down to the queueing mentality. Europeans seem obsessed with queueing and 'ownership' of spaces which they feel are rightly theirs through custom or usage. In the early morning rush hour, the main arterial roads are usually blocked whereas the back streets are relatively traffic-free. Drive to a local village or town and you will find cars parked on the outskirts when there is plenty of room available right in the centre. People who are positive thinkers and believe in their PSI power will experiment with the back routes and search for the short cuts. You won't find positive thinkers at the end of the queue. Nor will you find them particularly bothered about entering another person's 'space.' And just as the positive driver searches for short cuts and back routes in heavy traffic, you can do the same in the office promotion stakes and in your business activities. But before we go further into that, let me tell you about 'space' ownership. It is important to understand how much it means to some people who draw invisible boundaries.

A psychoanalyst friend of mine owns a beautiful fifteenth century farmhouse on the borders of Kent and Surrey about forty-five kilometers south of London. He spends weekends there but during the week he lives in central London. At one stage of his career he tried commuting, which involved taking the train from the village of Edenbridge to Victoria

Station, London. After the second or third day, he was standing on the platform at Edenbridge awaiting the train when a well-dressed man approached him and asked him to move away from the spot he occupied. Not believing his ears, the psychoanalyst politely but firmly asked the man why he was making this request.

The man's reply put an instant and premature end to my friend's commuting. 'I don't want you to stand there,' the man petulantly told my friend. 'I have been standing on that spot waiting for the train over a period of twenty years. It is my spot and nobody else is allowed to stand there. Everyone knows that! Now would you please move.' Space restrictions also applied inside the carriage on that particular train. If anyone dared sit in a seat normally used by a 'regular' the offender would be met with icy stares from other commuters. The man's actions told a lot about his character. He was conservative in his ways, a man of habit, petty-minded, and a stickler for rules and red tape. By 'reading' him correctly and treating him in a manner which would not threaten his ordinary and boring existence, you could turn him into a useful ally who would not let you down.

Are you an innovator or do you follow rules? Try this next quiz and see how you shape up. Answer the questions with either 'Yes,' 'Not sure,' or 'No.'

1. Do people compliment you on your sense of initiative?
2. Do you believe in the principle that rules are there to be obeyed?
3. Are you the creative type?
4. Do you tend to seek solutions along tried and tested lines?

5. Do you find yourself often challenging rules?
6. Are you more concerned with resolving problems than finding them?
7. Do you have little respect for past customs?
8. Are you capable of accurate and detailed work?
9. Are you confident that your ideas will usually work in practice?
10. Do you prefer to work with colleagues who never 'rock the boat'?
11. Do other people regard you as the impractical type?
12. Would you be happy working for a bureaucracy?
13. Are you always looking to delegate routine tasks?
14. Do you consider yourself to be the predictable type?
15. Do you think you have more 'flair' than your colleagues?

Scoring: First of all, give yourself 2 points for each 'Yes' answer, 1 point for 'Not sure' and 0 points for 'No.' Then add up your scores for odd and even numbered items separately. If you score more highly for the odd numbered items, then you are the innovative type. You tend to judge each case on its merits, to work from first principles, and avoid tedium and drudgery. You find it exciting to look for new solutions and you are always questioning rules and conventions. You are letting your PSI power take over in unknown situations and allowing positive feelings to win the day.

If you score more highly for the even numbered items, then you are a follower. You find life easier when there is a set routine to follow, and a standard way of doing things. You keep your energy for doing things along tried and tested paths. You cannot see the point of doing things differently just for the sake of it. From your point of view, traditional customs have a lot of sense behind them. You will use your PSI-FORCE effectively and cautiously but you are unlikely to take astral rides into the unknown.

Beat your boss

Everybody has it in them to outsmart their boss. Whether you are a young typist or secretary in your first job or a lowly paid tea boy or a budding executive, PSI power can be used to make you a winner. You can start climbing the ladder to success and outwit your boss at the same time! Here's how you do it.

Using PSI power and meditation and relaxation techniques already discussed, picture in your mind the office you work in or the job you do and think of the key individuals with whom you are involved. Stand apart from yourself and be the impartial onlooker who is assessing you and your colleagues. Now go over recent events in the office and list all your strong and weak points as well as making a summary of relationships among the staff, including yours. Be hard on yourself. Decide what role *you* play in your work situation and then determine what role you would like to play. Now turn the tables on yourself. Imagine *you* are the boss and see if the picture changes. In your imaginary role as the boss what do you think of you the employee? How do you see yourself and your prospects? Play as many role reversals as possible to give yourself the widest scope for self-analysis.

110

Next, begin analysing your boss. This may take several days or even a few weeks but it will be worth it in the end. Learn everything there is to know about him or her until you reach a stage where you can use mental telepathy to send images and receive them. Test yourself thoroughly. Once you reckon you know your boss, try and predict how he or she would react in given situations. Psych yourself to think like the boss thinks. Only by putting yourself on the same mental level will you be able to communicate telepathically. Once you have achieved this, let the boss know how you would react in response to a problem or situation before your boss has had time to think about it. If you were right and make a habit of this, you will soon be noticed not only by the boss but by other executive staff. The boss is always right!

At this stage, you can start planning some coups that neither the boss nor your colleagues will ever realise were intentional. Plan ahead and act on information you know will be reaching the boss and on which he or she will have to make a decision. Your chief will be dumbfounded when you inform him or her that the matter has already been taken care of in the correct manner. Make sure the board of directors knows what you have done. A lot of bosses take the credit for everything their junior executives or employees do. It's also a good idea to get friendly with the boss's secretary without making it too obvious. Good secretaries can be ideal links for getting through to the boss. They generally know their boss better than anybody else does.

The slave driver: If your boss is a slave driver who is only using your good services without giving you credit or offering improvement, you have several options for dealing with the situation. If you don't like the job and you think your chances of promotion are nil, start looking for another job without breaking your back to fulfill unreasonable demands. The worst thing you can do is allow yourself to become stressed and anxious as a result of the executive's behaviour.

If you want to stay in the job because you like it and think you may be promoted, use everything you have learned about the boss to bring about a desired change in attitude. If, for example, your boss has a sense of humour, you could suggest he or she gives you the office key. Such a request will obviously require an explanation, at which point in time you will have your chance to explain that, unless you stay at the office all night, there will be no hope of finishing your work to the high standard you are used to giving.

Explain to the boss that you value your pride in your job and that you want to give one hundred per cent of your efforts to ensure things are done properly. He or she will have to agree with this. Then tell the boss that if a proper job is required you will not be able to guarantee it because of the unreasonable work load. Explain that a second rate job could cost the company a lot of money and clients. This is an argument that cannot be ignored because you have introduced an anxiety factor – fear of losing money or business. Make sure you have all the right answers up your sleeve to any objections that may put up. Another factor which could influence the boss is the timing of your approach. Make sure the boss is in a relaxed and happy mood and open to suggestion. Make the approach at a time you think is most suitable. It might be after a good lunch or you could try early in the morning or after work and explain to the boss that you did not want to encroach on work time to sort out this problem. You could soon have your boss eating out of your hand!

The human machine: If your boss treats you as though you are part of the office furniture or an extension of the word processor, you must quickly point out the very big mistake your chief is making. Being regarded as a robot does very little for one's self-esteem but you can overcome this obstacle. You are *not* a robot but a human and therefore you can think and scheme and psych your way out of situations of this nature. The most effective way of doing this is by being so efficient at your work that your absence will immediately be noticed. Build up goodwill with other colleagues and executives so that they appreciate your valuable services. Make yourself indispensable for certain tasks and then when everyone, including the boss, is dependent on you, tell him what you think of the way you are being treated and explain that you might look elsewhere for another job which wants human beings. The threat of losing a good employee will not be taken lightly, especially if you are badly needed at this moment of time.

Don't be frightened to say 'No,' to your boss; be polite but be firm. Machines can't say 'No' but humans can, and if he or she imposes impossible tasks on you, refuse and explain why you have refused. You will be more respected for your refusal than if you had accepted ridiculous demands and failed to carry them out.

Once you have mastered an office or job skill, don't be content with continuing in the same job. Learn other skills to give yourself the opportunity of advancement into more responsible positions. Don't be frightened to take on different jobs just because you haven't learned them. Everyone has to make mistakes in the learning process. You will get more respect for trying and offering to extend yourself. And once you have mastered different skills you will be able to argue with the boss that the company is throwing away money by having you do mundane jobs when a person of your skill could be doing something far more productive and profitable.

The Romeo boss: Don't be victimised by the Romeo boss. If he doesn't own the company you are working for, he is walking on thin ice by taking liberties with you. He knows that but he doesn't think you know it. If his superiors get to hear of it he could be in trouble but it is in your interests to cool his ardour with the least possible damage to your own career. If you are married or live with someone, tell him how happy you are and what a wonderful man your husband or boyfriend is. Let him know that there is nobody who could replace your partner.

If you are not married or do not have a steady boyfriend, be honest with your boss. Tell him you are sorry but that you don't fancy him in the least. Assure him that if you did fancy him, you would be only too happy to accept his generous advances. If he persists, ask him if there is something wrong with his wife. Suggest to him that you could discuss his problem with his wife. Alternatively, ask him how he would feel if his wife or girlfriend was molested by her male colleagues. If he persists then you must act in a more positive manner. Tell him that the next time he puts a hand out of place you will have to report him because you can't do your job properly.

Take the initiative: You can psych your way to the top by building up your own image without the help of your boss or colleagues. I have had personal experience of this but must warn you that it could backfire if you are not careful. Nevertheless, the example I will give you illustrates how the principle works. A young cousin of mine was given a job by a large retail shopping empire during his university holidays. The store manager had taken an interest in him and hoped he would remain working for the chain rather than continuing his studies. My cousin had no intention of staying there however and thought he would play a managerial game. After all, he considered he had nothing to lose.

He was put into the cosmetics section where the department boss decided to teach him the trade from scratch. He was asked to stack soaps and cosmetics on the shelves as well as serving customers. My cousin found this too demeaning and instead walked around the store with his hands behind his back pretending to be the boss. He was immediately singled out for promotion by the other staff who, while despising him for not doing the mundane work, grudgingly admired him for acting like the boss and considered he had leadership qualities as a result. And despite complaints by his department boss, the store's manager offered him a permanent position with assurances of quick promotion. What my cousin had done was to psych his immediate boss with his positive, if somewhat cheeky approach. The boss did not know how to react to the situation and other workers accepted the role my cousin had created for himself.

The great divide: Status within an office can be a very carefully conceived plan of one-upmanship by an ambitious boss to give as much importance as the budget will allow him or her to get away with. The status-conscious boss will want to separate himself or herself as far as humanly possible from the rest of the staff. Further offices housing personal secretaries will also be created to provide an obstacle course preventing easy access to the boss. The main office will be plushly decorated and have a large desk which will dwarf the visitor. Don't be made to feel inferior with this kind of boss. Your PSI power is far more reliable and capable of giving *you* the upper hand than a piece of furniture which the boss is relying on to help build an image.

Walk into the office as if you own it. When you are offered a small chair in front of the desk, take a seat on the sofa and establish your own presence by acting the equal. Don't be frightened by the artificial trappings of importance.

Study your office design and use the knowledge to your advantage. If the office is open-plan, establish the location of the employees who are held in highest esteem by the boss. Try and place yourself next to them. Alternatively, if you are in a very large building with lots of space, try and arrange an office for yourself thereby creating an executive image. By acting important your collegues and bosses will eventually believe you are!

Winning at work:

1. Don't stay somewhere where you are not appreciated.
2. Don't be frightened to say 'No.'
3. Teach yourself every aspect of your particular job and then learn new skills. Make yourself indispensable at what you do.

116

4. Be positive with your boss. Behave as if you are an equal.
5. Don't get involved in arguments. Make your point and give reasons. Don't give excuses.
6. Don't be frightened of making decisions. No matter at what level you are, take the initiative.
7. Don't be a slave to your job. Do it well and efficiently but don't let it undermine your social and family life.
8. Listen to what colleagues and bosses have to say before committing yourself too readily.
9. If you find your work too stressful, change jobs or insist on having breaks which will improve your performance.
10. Don't take on extra work because you find it difficult to refuse.
11. Don't get bored in your job. If you are bored, look around for a new job or ask your boss if you can do other tasks.
12. Do the PSI meditation and relaxation exercises and study your colleagues and boss.
13. Devise a goal and then set about achieving it.
14. Don't be bullied by your boss. Form a plan of action which will get him off your back. This is best done by learning all his strengths and weaknesses.
15. Establish good relationships with your fellow workers. Treat work like a game. Use PSI power to help you discover your colleagues' inner selves and then play to win. Use your knowledge of communication and image building. You could soon be the boss!

Perfect your personal relationships with PSI power

One of the great strengths of PSI power is the everlasting bond it is capable of cementing between blood relatives and close friends. It forms part of the unspoken channel of communication between man and wife, parent and child, and kindred spirits. Often it ignores the boundaries of space and time, it continues beyond life and into death. Those who are close to you will never 'die.' Their physical presence may vanish but their spirit will remain with you forever more.

Relationships with loved ones do not always run a smooth course, no matter how deeply you feel for each other. I firmly believe that friendships should never be permanently wrecked. For this reason, it is important to understand differences of opinion and to come to terms with them through the medium of PSI. Why live a life of despair when with a little thought and effort you can make your lot a happy one? If you work on it, your personal happiness will reach unknown peaks and the benefits you will derive will spread to other areas of your existence.

An understanding of those closest to you is the key to this success. But first you must come to terms with yourself. Know your real self. What are *your* beliefs and values, your standards and aims, your strengths and weaknesses? What motivates you? What sort of person are you? I hope by now that you are beginning to understand your real self through PSI and the various tests I have asked you to do. In knowing yourself, you will be in a better position to understand why your actions produce different behaviour patterns in the people with whom you come into contact.

Here is a further test to help evaluate your real self. It determines if you like getting your own way. Answer the questions honestly with a 'Yes,' 'Not Sure,' or 'No.'

1. Are you at your happiest when telling others what to do?
2. Do you often find yourself to be the leader when in a group?
3. Do you enjoy arguing your own point of view?
4. Are you good at settling arguments for other people?
5. Do you often find yourself giving advice to friends and other people?
6. Can you usually talk your wife, other members of your family, or friends round to your point of view?
7. Do people often look to you for advice?
8. If you are on a committee, say at a school or social club, would you enjoy being in charge?
9. Do you sometimes find you have a powerful influence on others?
10. Are you good at getting your own way when it suits you?
11. Do you enjoy persuading others?
12. Do you consider it an important principle to stand up for your rights?
13. Do you enjoy questioning public speakers?
14. Do other people consider you the manipulative type?
15. Have you often got into trouble for speaking your mind too openly?

Scoring: Give yourself 2 points for each 'Yes' answer, 1 point for 'Not Sure' and 0 points for 'No.'

A score of 12 or more points suggests that you are a person who has a basic need to dominate others. You tend to be the assertive type, wanting to win others around to your own point of view. You are also the sort of person who will win an argument. A score of 18 points or more means you are a born leader. With your drive you should go far, but you must be careful not to be too dominating at home and with friends. Unless your partner and friends are content with playing second fiddle they will resent your inclination to be Number One.

A score of 11 or less indicates that you tend to be a follower rather than a leader. You might want to reserve your judgment in important matters before speaking your mind and when you do so you could well find that it is your opinion that is given most weight, even though you are not assertive in giving it.

Marriage

This is one of the most formidable institutions in the human race. It has created dynasties and kingdoms, it has brought unimaginable happiness and deepest despair. It has caused lasting feuds, inspired centuries of poetry, created life and destroyed life. It has aroused every emotion known to man, it has fed an army of lawyers, it has been embodied in the unwritten tribal law of primitive races and written into the statutes and case law of modern societies. Today, under Islamic law, an unfaithful wife can still be sentenced to death by stoning and in western society, a man can be dispossessed of much of his property through divorce proceedings. And despite all this, many people still wander into marriage without proper thought and often with very little advice or instruction. It is the one contract where allowances are made for the heart, rather than for the brain. If it later turns sour we can select, from millions of words written about the subject, an appropriate and pithy maxim like that noted by William Congreve (1670–1729) the Restoration playwright:

'Thus grief still treads upon the heels of pleasure: Marry'd in haste, we may repent at leisure.'

PSI power coupled with good practical sense could help *you* choose the right partner, and if you are married, assist you in overcoming problems within your relationship.

Choosing a partner: Love may be blind but your inner PSI power is not and you must have the good sense to rely on it to help you choose as best you can. Both you and your partner are making the biggest commitment of your lives and it is in your interests that you make the right decision.

Explore your inner minds together. See how well you 'read' each other's thoughts. Do you think the same way? Be honest with yourselves and learn what each of you is really like. Find out if your views on religion are similar. Are your attitudes to life and your aims compatible? What are your attitudes towards sex? Do you like the same things in sex? Do you enjoy sex together? One of the biggest stumbling blocks to a happily married life can result from sexual problems.

Are you happy with your partner's looks? Are you happy with each other's status and prospects and intelligence? If there is a considerable age difference between you, then a strong factor in your choice of partner may be the high esteem the younger partner has for the older. That could present problems over the years as the younger partner matures and develops his or her own skills thereby devaluing the admiration felt for the other's skills.

Psych yourselves to discover the reasons *why* you want to marry your partner. If it is for just one reason, say looks or money, circumstances or fortunes may alter that in the future. If you are both very young, you may develop into quite different people as you mature. Find out if you both want children and what your attitudes are to the in-laws. Do you already regard the in-laws as outlaws?

If both of you are going to work, will your proposed marriage be an equal partnership or does the domineering partner want to be boss? How would you handle this? What chores would each of you undertake in this marriage? If both of you are born leaders and are the type to win arguments, watch out. The arguments may never be won or lost but continue throughout your marriage. What happens if suddenly the career prospects of the female partner soar above that of the male partner? Will he feel his traditional role threatened? Will he cope?

Has either of you an overwhelming interest or passion which may eventually lead to an over-indulgence of this interest and a neglect of the other party? Sports widows can be just as unhappy as war widows.

It is questions like these that each partner must answer truthfully. Once your passion has been quelled by the passage of time, other factors must remain to make your marriage happy and stable. Above all, an understanding of each other and good communication, using all your PSI skills, is an essential ingredient to a happy future.

The PSI power way to a happy marriage is not to resist your natural impulses and thoughts but to understand them in relation to your inner self. In my opinion it is not wrong, once you are married, to desire other people. That is a natural impulse and one I have felt on many occasions. As I have already said, as a young man I enjoyed many relationships with beautiful women but finally, I realised that I needed a true and permanent love. I was fortunate enough to meet Hanna and we realised that what we had was something wonderful and stable at the same time. We were married in Mexico where we have a home and both of us are sure that our relationship will last forever.

Although we went through a ceremony, we don't feel the need for a piece of paper to tell us we are together. Our relationship is one of love, respect, affection and friendship. We feel we are lucky to have two beautiful and happy children.

Even so I am still a man. I have not lost a basic desire for other women just because I am married. I personally do not know any man who is not interested or does not desire other women just because he is married. We all like variety in our life even if we do not admit to wanting to be unfaithful. The important thing is that love must be made to grow in marriage and not fade out. But how do you do that?

From a sexual point of view – how many times can you eat rice every day of your life? We are animals and we cannot control our sexual passions. Our desires fade with the same partner. Inevitably, we want to try something else. But if you know the secret of balancing your desire then you can control your animal passions. Don't be obsessed with sex.

Keep a certain distance and leave intervals between making love so it does not become boring. Find out new ways of loving and give each other little surprises. Play love games together and then have periods of abstention. That will help keep alive your sexual interest. Remember too, that your safest sexual partner is the person you know and love and trust.

Growing together: As your marriage progresses, both of you will experience changes of a personal, physical, and professional nature. If one partner becomes career-minded, the other may aspire towards increasing the family; conflicts are likely to arise. Although these changes are regularly taking place, you will nevertheless be able to cope with them adequately, providing that communication between you is good.

You and your partner should undertake meditation together and talk to each other about your inner feelings and moods. Stay on the same wavelength. Don't allow misunderstandings to develop into long silences and a complete break-down in communication. Empathise with what the other partner is going through. Transmit positive thoughts and good feelings to one another.

Children and PSI: Life can seem very unfair on us at times. Some people experience as much heartache in their attempts to have children as others have controlling their too easily conceived but errant offspring.

For those unfortunate people who have difficulty in conceiving, I offer hope through PSI. For there is hope! I know of couples who have been told by doctors that they will not be able to conceive but who have confounded the medical experts. Don't lose hope. Be positive. Medical reports often show that 'childless' couples who adopted their first baby or had it through artificial insemination by donor (AID), were later able to conceive their very own child. Such is the positive power of PSI and love.

Only people who experience extreme problems in having a child, or those close to them, can fully appreciate the anguish suffered. Couples in this situation will sometimes move heaven and earth to achieve their aim. Psi power can help them greatly in coming to terms with their situation. It takes great understanding and power of the mind for an infertile husband to accept another man as the father of his wife's child. Yet if he allows his inner self to fully accept such a baby, he will be fully rewarded in time; the baby will grow up to be *his* baby. It will adopt all the physical mannerisms of the mother and 'father' and with positive thought it would be impossible, unless told otherwise, for the public to know it was not his very own baby.

The same can be said of an infertile mother who asks a surrogate to have her husband's child. Through positive PSI power, that child will be no different than if it were her own. Again, there are numerous cases of couples who have had a baby of their own after their first was conceived by a surrogate.

Crisis in marriage: Throughout marriage, you will find times when there are crises. It may be experienced early when you think you have made a mistake with the man or woman you married. Alternatively, it may consist of depression and anxiety or there may be sexual tension between you. At various stages we reach a mid-life crisis and menopause. Compassion and care must then be given but achieving this should already be within your grasp through an understanding of communication and inner reflection. Look for the positives and don't let negativism enter your relationship. Don't regret your yesterdays.

Affairs

I cannot act as a moral guardian for anybody about to embark on an affair. But I can ask them to consider all the elements involved and to reflect on their inner selves and question if it is a wise move. Positive thinking and PSI power should help you to determine the consequences of such activities.

If you are married with children and are having an affair with someone in a similar position, think of how many people you could be affecting. Your spouse, the other husband or wife, two sets of children, your friends and the friends of your lover; and that is just the beginning. It may spread to work colleagues and neighbours and your employers. Ask yourself why you are having the affair. Is it just a quick fling for sexual gratification or is it to boost your own ego? Is it out of revenge for your partner or are you simply unhappy in your marriage and looking for someone else to love?

Having asked yourself the reasons, look at the consequences if you are found out. Question whether the affair is worth all the trouble it may give you if you are. Is the other man or woman more important to you than your husband or wife and family? Because you may have to give them up. How compatible a person is your lover? Could you live as happily with your lover as you could with your wife or husband and would the romance die if you were married to each other? Perhaps even more importantly, if he or she plays around now, what does the future hold? Is it likely to happen again with someone different?

PSI and the love cheats: There is a high rate of cheating among lovers in our society despite the alarming risk of contracting serious infectious sexual diseases which can, as in the case of AIDS, be fatal. I would urge everyone to choose their sexual partner with the greatest possible care and always keep in mind that limiting sex to one partner is the safest way to minimise the risk of contracting harmful diseases.

If you suspect your partner has or is engaging in extramural sex, you may choose to ignore it or to have a confrontation, if only to put your mind at ease. Whatever course of action you pursue, your knowledge of PSI will help you ascertain the facts. Here's what you do. Relax your body and mind and concentrate on your partner. He or she has been behaving differently lately and there has been some guilt which you have been able to detect from your inner PSI senses. Transfer your thought patterns to your partner and see how he or she reacts. Touch your partner and 'read' the reaction. Has it changed from before? Does your partner's speech pattern differ? Has their body language changed?

If you are sure that your partner has had illicit sex, try to ascertain if it is a regular feature, a one-off, a holiday romance, or an occasional fling. You may react in different ways depending on how serious you consider your partner's transgression.

The holiday affair: Ask yourself if this is going to be a regular feature or a one-off. Will it really affect you so much if it is a one-off? Do you really want to let him or her know? Perhaps you could try and discuss with your partner the hypothetical case of having a holiday romance. You could ask the offending partner if he or she would mind if *you* had a romance with someone else on holiday. How would your partner feel about it? From the response, you should be able to draw conclusions as to how far to take this conversation or whether to stop at this point and never again mention the affair.

A one-off fling: I would question the wisdom of jeopardising everything you have for the sake of a moment's passion which afterwards is meaningless. Sexual desire is a natural and basic urge and there are moments when all of us are weak. If you are tempted, your own will-power should be strong enough to resist. If your partner is in tune with you, he or she should be able to tell whether or not you have resisted or taken the forbidden fruit. If you are the innocent party I do not think a one-off fling is serious enough to destroy a good marriage. If you love your partner, be confident enough to tell yourself that he or she really is in love with you and that it will never happen again.

The affair: If your partner is having a serious affair then you must use every effort in determining what has gone wrong with your own relationship. An established affair, unless it is with your blessing, is rarely a healthy sign of a good marriage. If you know the other person your partner is involved with, PSI recognition will probably tell you immediately if they are more than just good friends. Watch for signs of body language, particularly eye contact and verbal communication. Once you have established the affair, tell your partner that you want to discuss it without getting too angry or upset.

Psych yourself for the confrontation. Tell yourself you will not get emotional or irrational but that you will talk this problem out in a sensible manner. Discover the reasons behind the affair. Tell yourself it is not worth becoming emotionally upset because there will be nothing to gain from a negative attitude. Be receptive to your partner's explanation, even if you do not sympathise with it. Explain your feelings and tell your partner what you think the two of you should do about it. Suggest independent advice if he or she is not willing to listen to you.

Open marriages: This type of marriage seems doomed from the outset, because it is usually imposed by one partner on the other and inevitably leads to jealousy and hostilities. I know an eminently qualified doctor who was married to his former nurse and both of them agreed to a liberal life-style where either could sleep with other partners. It was the husband's idea. He told me he would feel less guilty about his own affairs if he told his wife she had *carte blanche* to sleep with other men. Eventually he began feeling jealous because of her immense popularity with a number of his colleagues. The pair finally split up and the doctor is a very unhappy man. He feels he has lost a wife who was a wonderful lover and person. Originally, she did not want to sleep with other men but was persuaded by her love for her husband. Neither had used the PSI approach to discover their inner feelings. If they had, the pair might have been more honest with each other and the doctor's foolishness in 'forcing' his wife into something she did not want to do would have prevented the unhappy outcome.

129

Children: Develop a good and healthy relationship with your children through PSI. A close and happy relationship can be possible if you are aware of the changing cycle of your child's life. The early formative years see many changes as does the period when your child reaches puberty and looks forward to independence. Use the techniques of communication to effectively discuss problems which arise and advise rather than channel your child in a particular direction.

Understanding your own motives in the advice you give can be a helpful indicator. Be sure that your advice is not a result of your own frustrations or disappointments. If you wanted to be a doctor but your parents could not afford it, then don't force that ambition on your child. It could be a recipe for disaster.

Examine your attitude to your child's friends and ask yourself whether the restrictions you put on your child are reasonable. If your child rebels against you, search your inner self to see if you have been in any way responsible for such feelings.

Communicate with your children as much as possible. Teach them to approach you if they have fears or worries about coping with certain aspects of life, particularly drugs. Learn when to say nothing at all but to listen to your child. Discuss your own fears with your child and point out the danger of experimenting with things like drugs. If they ask you about sex, tell them what you think they should know. Warn them especially of the dangers of promiscuity in today's society. Tell them all about AIDS and other sexual diseases. But also try and relax with them and then discuss your innermost thoughts with each other. Above all, show your child that you can be a friend.

Avoid, if possible, having fights in front of the children. If you do argue or fight in front of them, then make sure that the children are present when you make up again. Let them see and hear you say sorry to each other. Let them witness you having a make-up kiss. Explain to them that love has its differences and that despite everything you do still love each other, and them, and that you are sorry for what happened.

Divorce: If your marriage reaches a stage where you feel there is no point in continuing and you are intent on divorce, use all you have learned to make an effective break. Forget the circumstances leading to the break. Accept that they have happened and that it is no longer necessary to rekindle hurtful memories. Be positive. You must now look forward and if you are in any way negative, it will make matters worse for you and your partner.

Before talking to your partner about the break, relax and meditate. Tell yourself that you are going to be firm and positive and that you will not become angry or emotional when discussing the subject of divorce. Choose an appropriate time when neither of you is under pressure. Suggest your partner relaxes with you. Tell him or her that what you want will be the best for both of you. Ask your partner's help. Put yourself outside of the relationship and act as though you are helping another couple come to terms with their break-up. Make it as friendly as you possibly can. There is no point in getting involved in costly litigation and ending up losing half your proceeds to the lawyers.

Be fair about dividing your assets and allowing access to the children. Make sure that when you break the news to your children, you do so together.

Reassure your children that both of you love them and that it is not their fault. Explain to them the reasons for your marriage break-down and tell your children that it won't affect your feelings for them. Tell them what will happen now that you are going to part and be positive about the future. Let them see the positive side of your separation.

Death: Marriage, divorce, moving house, and death are just four of the main crisis periods in our lives. It is within us all to fight the negative attitudes that prevail in these times of extreme stress. Death is as much a part of our existence as birth. We begin dying the second we are born and we must all come to terms with that. The last thing our loved ones would wish is for us to ruin our own lives with grief as a result of their departure. A period of mourning is healthy, providing it does not continue and overshadow our normal day to day life. Think to yourself how lucky you were to have the friendship and love of the person who has died. Look on the positive side of your friend's or partner's death. They may have been in constant pain and were looking for an escape. Their life, even if it ended prematurely, may have been an extremely happy or fulfilling one.

Continuing to grieve for an excessive period of time is self-indulgent and negative. No good will come of it. You are doing a disservice to yourself and to others and you have a duty to yourself to make the best of your life. Give yourself positive PSI thoughts. Say to yourself: 'I am lucky to be alive. Life is good and enjoyable. My friend would have wanted me to enjoy myself. We are not apart from each other forever. I can feel my friend's presence. I always will. I can still talk to my friend. His departure, though permanent, is in other ways no different from the separation we feel from friends who are thousands of miles away.'

Believe me, this positive PSI thought *will* make you happier and help you to overcome your grief. I have had many personal experiencs of psychic happenings when friends of mine have died. It has helped me to live with the fact that I shall no longer see them in this life. Other experiences I can tell you about have been told to me by friends and I want to share some of these with you.

A close friend who was a jazz musician was dying of cancer. He could not readily accept this fact and asked me for reassurance in his final days. I spoke to him about some of the happy experiences others had told me about when they were near to death and I urged him not to be frightened. We grew very close and just when I felt I was getting through to him and that he was resigned to his fate, we both heard a dog bark. We looked, but there was no dog around. Yet both of us had heard a dog bark. My friend looked at me and said: 'Uri, they are coming for me.' That same night, about ten, I was at home and the lights in my house went out. I turned to Shipi and said: 'Don has died. This is a sign from him.' The next morning his wife rang me to say her husband was dead. I told her I knew. 'He died last night at ten.' She was overwhelmed but the thought that there had been communication somehow helped her get through her own grief and unhappiness.

Another friend of mine, a publisher, told me he wanted to die because he was old and sick and his wife had died some months earlier. He only wanted one person to attend his funeral, a lady who lived in Paris. At his invitation she came to London and his power was such that he died virtually an hour after she had been with him. I told Shipi that this man had such a powerful sense of PSI that he was bound to communicate his temporal passing. I was not disappointed. The moment he died we heard a peck on the window and opened it. A sparrow flew inside. He was letting us know.

How can you feel continuous grief when there is communication of this sort? I knew my friend was happy. He died as he had lived. He was fully in control until the very end.

Some of my very close relatives who have died are still with me in my thoughts almost every day. Particularly my father and grandmother. I don't feel they have left me at all. They are still as vibrant and real to me today as when they were alive. Death has only deprived me of their physical presence.

Many widows I have spoken to were convinced they could not survive without their husbands. Yet, within a short time, they have been able to re-organise their lives. They have taken up educational courses, established new friends, and even travelled round the world. They have found a different kind of happiness which in its own way was just as fulfilling as when they were married. Yet initially they experienced despair and loneliness. Their positive attitude however, soon pulled them out of it, and they were able to make a fresh start.

I think the most positive of all comments I ever heard about death was from a five times married widow in Las Vegas. She cheerfully told me about her many husbands who, she insisted, she had loved as dearly as each other. 'I know they were happy,' she told me. 'They all died with smiles on their faces.'

You can be rich and successful

At the north end of Westminster Palace which houses the British Parliament, there is a three hundred and twenty foot high clock-tower, universally and affectionately known as Big Ben. It chimes the quarter hours on four bells and the hours are struck on a huge bell weighing over thirteen tons, named after Sir Benjamin Hall, First Commissioner of Works when the clock was erected. It is my intention, as I write this book, to one day bring that clock to a dead stop. I will choose my moment carefully because I do not want to damage British heritage. I want only to prove to people that if you have enough faith you can do the 'impossible.'

I also want to make it clear that I do not need this challenge to 'prove' myself. In financial terms, I have already made it; I am a millionaire several times over and I could stop work this very minute without ever altering my lifestyle. But like every other successful person, I feel the need for achieving goals, no matter how high those might be. Furthermore, it's fun. Like many other millionaires, I enjoy the chase more than the kill. Getting rich can be similar to playing an enjoyable game and the rewards at the end become a pleasing by-product.

I want to share my own secrets with you so that *you* too can be a winner. Being successful does not mean you have to make a million. You can climb the ladder of success in small or large businesses, be amply rewarded for your efforts, and enjoy yourself at the same time. And you will certainly have all the material comforts you need without breaking your neck to become super-rich. I believe everybody can be wealthy and successful if they put their minds to it. Getting there depends on your attitude. You may be surprised to hear this but most millionaires I have met don't like talking about money. I believe their interest lies in the exciting real life games they play in achieving their goals. Money is secondary to this. Have you ever played the game of 'Monopoly'? I think most of us have at some time or another. Wasn't it much more fun playing the game and winning rather than laboriously counting your money?

It is still possible to fulfill the rags to riches dream in the West. A lot of people have done it and others are still doing it. I did it myself! I know three Israeli brothers who arrived destitute in New York, slept in subways and then formed one of the most successful jeans businesses in America. They are now multi-millionaires. It requires guts and work and positive thoughts. And it's there if you want it. Try this next quiz to assess your level of ambition. Answer the questions with a 'Yes,' 'Not Sure,' or 'No.'

1. Are you at your happiest when striving after things?
2. Do you think the main purpose of life is to achieve something important?
3. Do other people regard you as the ambitious type?
4. Would you love to write a novel?
5. Are you always setting goals for yourself?
6. Do you often daydream of accomplishing something of great significance?
7. Do you feel a sense of satisfaction after finishing a hard task?

8. Do you almost always give of your best?
9. Is it your ambition in life to be recognised for something?
10. Do you particularly enjoy puzzles and crosswords?
11. Is doing things better than other people important to you?
12. Do you hate to give up even when success looks impossible?
13. Even when playing games for fun, do you have to win?
14. Do you have to succeed even if others are hurt in the process?

Scoring: Give yourself 2 points for every 'Yes' answer, 1 point for 'Not Sure,' and 0 points for 'No.'

A score of 17 or more points indicates that you are the ambitious type. You have a powerful need to achieve and an underlying force that gives purpose to your life. You are unlikely to be happy unless you have something to aim at each day. In the extreme, you are in danger of becoming a workaholic!

If you have the natural ingredients for becoming successful, then your knowledge of PSI power should be of considerable help in channelling your energies and concentration to that end. PSI-FORCE will give you the positive attitude you need. Through PSI meditation, it will also allow you to reflect and concentrate on your future and the goals you wish to achieve. You may have the means to achieve your goals but without proper direction you may miss out.

My own experience is relevant in discussing this point. As a young man, I was making an extremely good living by giving performances of metal bending and other PSI phenomena. I could make as much as five thousand dollars a night by using my talents. Over a fortnight, I was assured of at least fifty thousand dollars. Yet the same talents, applied in another direction over the same timescale, made my fortune of millions of dollars. Why? Because somebody pointed out to me that I should take a different, and more profitable direction. They showed me another target which could use my special skills in a similar way but bring me far greater rewards.

The person responsible for that was the head of a multinational company, and it is thanks to him that I am so wealthy today. I first met the late Sir Val Duncan at a party in 1973, and he showed great interest in my psychic powers. He was chairman of the giant Rio-Zinc Corporation as well as a director of the Bank of England, and I immediately sensed that here was a man of vision who was not afraid to experiment with the powers of the mind. His own interest in PSI and its potential, was far more crystallised than my own. Sir Val was an amateur dowser and had seen the financial implications of finding precious metals and oil through PSI. He figured companies could wipe tens of millions of dollars off their exploration budget if they ignored expensive traditional means of exploration and used PSI instead. Unfortunately, his fellow board directors were not so open-minded about these possibilities.

At his invitation, I visited Sir Val in London and also at his Spanish holiday retreat on the island of Majorca. There, Sir Val began teaching me all he knew about dowsing. It was a lot of fun. Sir Val would hide jewellery and olive oil around his garden and invite me to take part in a treasure hunt. In fact he was testing my powers. Once I was able to detect the whereabouts of all these objects with a high degree of success, we progressed from there to finding real 'treasure' – mineral wealth – by just using maps.

'Uri,' he finally said to me one day. 'I think it is now time that you stopped thinking about the few thousand dollars that you can make at performances and concentrate on millions. You have to change direction and diversify your powers.' As with all new things we make mistakes. My initial mistake involved giving away a lot of advice for free and making millions for some very large companies around the world, who found minerals where I predicted they would be but did not pay me a penny. I considered that to be a positive lesson. It was no use crying about lost income. Next time, I said, I would make sure I had legal contracts before helping companies with their explorations.

Working with a good lawyer to represent you (and be sure to get at least two sound recommendations before you make your choice) is extremely important. Indeed, I cannot emphasise this too much. Also, you should aim to structure your fee arrangements with the lawyer so he or she gets paid by results. Working with your lawyer in this way can make all the difference if your legal adviser has direct interest in ensuring your venture is properly protected, and your work fully rewarded.

Over the past ten years I have travelled the world for large mining companies giving my expertise in locating minerals. I have dowsed for gold and oil from small aircraft above the Amazon jungles and as far away as the Solomon Islands. Mr Peter Sterling, who runs the Australian mining company Zanex Ltd in Melbourne, approached me in 1985 to act as a consultant in his search for minerals on the remote Solomon Islands in the south Pacific more than a thousand miles north east of Australia. Since then it has been widely reported how I was invited to the opening of Zanex's Mavu mine.

Peter Sterling was delighted with my work. He said I had shortened the odds of finding minerals from some three hundred to one to about one in three. I was also given a testimonial from the company's director. It stated: 'I confirm that Zanex is about to commence exploration in areas identified by you in Solomon Islands. The most interesting area identified to date is on Malaita Island where upon your instructions we are about to commence a search for gold and diamonds. We have already confirmed the presence of Kimberlite which could be diamondiferous in this area. Other areas will be investigated in due course.'

Through my friendship with the powerful Japanese Aoki Corporation's chief, John Aoki, and John Tishman of the United States' Tishman Realty, I was instrumental in setting up a multi-million dollar skyscraper development in California. My own business interests now range from property to publishing, electronic inventions, manufacturing, fashion and games. One of my successful games has been 'Uri Geller's STRIKE', which Matchbox toys have sold around the world, and I am always adding new ventures to my list of successes.

All it requires is positive thinking, energy and proper channelling of mind power. And once you are there and have achieved financial independence, you can take it easy without the stress accompanied by a busy life. I personally tend to relax quite a lot and spend much of my time doing physical exercise. I became a millionaire before I was thirty and now, each time another million is notched up, Shipi and I celebrate with a bottle of champagne and note the date we did it. With the offers that I have received, I could be far richer than I am, but money for the sake of accumulating wealth is not my priority.

A lot of rich people are criticised because the public

thinks they are super-greedy and that they amass wealth to the detriment of others. I happen to think the opposite. I think entrepreneurs actually create a lot of jobs and bring wealth to other people and I further believe that it is the playing and winning they like rather than the spoils.

Take Robert Strauss, head of Australia's huge Bridge Oil Company. He told me recently he was more excited by the challenge of 'achieving the impossible'. This was much more important to him, he said, than making more money.

Look at the way Saul Steinberg, founder of the American company Leasco and chairman of Reliance Holdings, sees himself. Popularly labelled as 'The King of Wall Street,' Steinberg claims he is one of the richest men in the world. He looks on his activities as someone who enjoys a bloodless battle: 'My business life is a way of going to war without killing anyone.' The Brooklyn-born money-man started his astronomical career at nineteen, when he borrowed 300 thousand dollars and took over a local timber company. Since then he has built an empire involving computers, property and insurance and estimates his assets as in the region of 3.7 billion dollars. He has a simple reason for continuing his 'war games,' despite his immense wealth. He says: 'I find business relaxing.' But the key to his empire was getting 'bank finance.'

Remember what I said about how to deal with your bank manager? About building up good credit lines and establishing yourself as a worthy risk? Whether you have an established business base or you are just starting out, the principle is the same. If you don't have the money it is impossible to expand in a big way without borrowing extra funds.

As a young man, Rupert Murdoch, the international

newspaper and TV magnate, inherited the *Adelaide News*, an evening newspaper in South Australia's capital city. It was considered to be a good 'money spinner' but did not have the powerful base of the bigger newspaper groups in the major cities of Sydney and Melbourne. Young Rupert could have lived a supremely comfortable life tucked away in a mansion in the Adelaide hills or stayed among the Melbourne social set where he grew up. Instead, he hocked his assets to the bank and began borrowing on a massive scale, first buying up newspapers in Sydney and then in other capital cities.

Stretched for money after he had opened a New York office, he was asked by one of his top Australian executives what restrictions would be imposed in the bureau's news office. His positive reply, instantly delivered, became part of the legend that surrounds him today: 'Go nowhere, cover everything, pay nothing,' said the budding tycoon.

Whereas competitors thought Murdoch had overstretched the mark and that his newspapers would fail, his organisation went from strength to strength. As his empire grew, so did his borrowing. He expanded his purchases to New Zealand, Hong Kong, Britain and America, eventually becoming a US citizen.

He is personally one of the mega-rich but still owes millions and millions of dollars to banks and governments for his new acquisitions. Despite his fortune, he has never forgotten his old bank manager friend from Adelaide who set him on the road to his global take-overs by lending him money to buy a newspaper in Sydney. The manager, now retired, is still taken out to lunch or invited to dinner when Rupert is back in town.

I view Rupert Murdoch as one of the world's most gifted communicators. As a businessman he has few equals. But how can one man run a world-wide network as he does and yet make his presence felt so that junior executives tremble when he jets in for a brief visit to one of his many and varied enterprises?

The key to this is his choice of top executives. Murdoch has an uncanny knack of choosing the right man. He has an instinctive feel about his staff which comes about from his PSI gifts as a communicator. Using his PSI power he can instantly read people and knows whether they will be up to the job. Then he makes sure that he is in constant communication with them no matter where he is. Unlike some multinationals, where executives are not known to the chairman, Murdoch remembers the first name and details of all his top executives. His own enthusiasm for his enterprises sparks off an electric telepathy into those working for him with obvious beneficial results which make ecstatic balance sheet reading for his investors!

Virgin Records boss, Richard Branson was only eighteen when he began his business empire which is now a multi-million dollar multinational concern. He has used PSI communication with astounding results. Rather than alienate himself from the enterprising young team he employed, he continued to live aboard his modest houseboat on a canal in London's Little Venice area for many years, wheeling and dealing from his cabin office and writing memos in Biro on his hands and knees, while looking every inch the casual bearded, jeans-wearing drop-out of the 60s. His great key to success was being 'in touch' with the young which helped him sign up people like Boy George of Culture Club and hugely successful artists like Mike Oldfield. Branson is a whizz-kid businessman who, through proper use of communication techniques, can inspire and enthuse others.

Often you will find an aura exists around powerful and influential people. In PSI terms this signifies a spiritual development or a form of radiation about that person's body. I believe certain people acquire this aura after years of self improvement through the medium of PSI. They have sharpened their senses and their basic talents and the aura becomes a manifestation of their success.

In 1985 I was invited to the fiftieth birthday party of Adnan Kashoggi, one of the most powerful men in the Arab world. Guests arrived in the manner expected at such a lavish occasion, either in Rolls Royces or Mercedes or by helicopter. Some had sailed to Marbella in their yachts and were airlifted to Adnan's luxury villa nearby. Show-business guests like Brooke Shields and Sean Connery were feted by the rich and the beautiful. But few had the aura I sensed around Adnan himself.

He was a man who could control his facial movements but his eyes flashed with communication and intelligence. He was a man whose PSI instinct had proved as unbeatable as his bank balance, which could be measured in billions rather than millions.

According to those who know both men, Adnan is very similar in his PSI make-up to Mahdi Al-Tajir, a Bahrain carpet merchant's son who also measures his wealth in billions. Al-Tajir went on a property buying spree in Britain and in one year purchased estates worth about $50 million. He was chosen as ambassador to London for the United Arab Emirates after a humble start in life as a customs officer in Dubai. Apart from his diplomatic duties he is also a financial adviser to Dubai's powerful Sheikh Rashid.

The will to 'prove' himself was very strong when Sir James Goldsmith was still a boy. He was teased at Eton, Britain's school for the aristocracy, for being half-Jewish. But his 'I'll show 'em' positive thinking has paid dividends. From his base in America, he controls a multi-million dollar empire which is growing from strength to strength. His PSI determination made him headline news when he was just twenty: he ran off with his seventeen year old wife, Isobel Patino, heiress to a $100,000,000 Bolivian tin fortune.

The most legendary of all millionaires, Howard Hughes, would probably have been a superb psychic. He was a man whose power of positive thought held few limitations. Hughes' strength lay in his PSI power. No challenge was too small or too great. He would turn his hand to aeroplanes, designing oil drills, or creating women's brassieres with the same non-defeatist attitude as he would attack the rest of his business dealings. As his psychic awareness increased, so did his attractiveness to women. His aura of PSI success had aphrodisiac qualities.

Among his few equals were men like Aristotle Onassis and John Paul Getty, neither of whom were as handsome or 'glamorous' as Hughes but nevertheless shared an indefinable aura that is so irresistible to women. They also had a vision of the future and were powerful and forceful enough to realise it.

It is also possible to work within a corporate structure and achieve outstanding success. Those people who do, however, require tremendous strength of character to overcome red-tape and company constrictions.

In 1986, the world saw the biggest ever share flotation of a nationalised industry – the 7.8 billion dollar sale of British Gas. The man behind the company, while keeping a low public profile, has a larger than life image within the industry and government circles, amounting to what I consider to be a super PSI strength of character. He is Sir Denis Rooke, the chairman, who was actually against the privatisation. A lesser figure would have been retired early or gently promoted sideways. Not Sir Denis. Working from the soundest base within a company's infrastructure – he knows more than anyone else and could do it better – he was able to push for improvements and innovations through sheer force of personality. And his vision for the industry has been justified with resounding results.

The son of a South London commercial traveller, he joined British Gas as an assistant engineer in 1949 after serving five years in the army. The lesson he learned in the military was: 'What you need is for everyone to agree on a course and then go and do it. If you do that you win. If you don't, you lose.' He pioneered the world's first shipment of two thousand tons of liquefied natural gas across the Atlantic, braving gale force storms with his dangerous experimental cargo. Colleagues thought they would never see their rising executive again and plotted his course with pessimism. But his vision paid off, proving the technology for commercial imports of Algerian natural gas. He made a future of an industry that had been forecast by the British Treasury as having no future.

His positive approach to life and his confidence in himself and his ability has led to him bullying government ministers, criticising the Queen's speech, and opposing the Chancellor of the Exchequer. It has won him grudging respect. His own staff admire him because every fitter in the works feels that he could do the job better than themselves. He has not rested on his laurels. He says of himself: 'I've never met anyone who couldn't be improved, who couldn't do a job better. And I think that of myself.'

Winning ways

Whether you want to go into business on your own or climb the corporate ladder as an executive, there are ways of winning the game. I believe the PSI way of winning is as effective if not more than other ways.

The positive you: Psych yourself to be positive. You must believe you are a winner. Say to yourself: 'I can pull off this business deal if I really want to. I have the skill and the knowledge. There is nothing that can stop me. I'm going to do it. I want to do it.'

Prepare yourself for any prospective deal as if you were going into a battle. Lay out your battle plans. Get your body and your mind into gear. Plan a bloodless coup. You can win and still be popular!

If it's a promotion you are after, win the confidence of your boss and the respect of your fellow workers. Start doing the job you're going after. Show the boss through your communication techniques that you're the man for the job.

Decision making: Don't be frightened to make a decision. If you are, you'll never be given the opportunity of even making a wrong one! Have faith in yourself. Be confident. Go through all the possibilities before you make your decision but then be firm about it. Right or wrong your reasons will be impeccable.

Time Wasters: Through PSI communication techniques, determine who you want to spend time talking with and whose company you can do without. Time is a precious and irretrievable commodity. Don't waste time talking unless it is going to do something for you. Don't waste time doing trivial things. Ask yourself if what you are doing is effective. If it is not leave it alone.

Delegation: Don't be frightened of delegating lesser tasks to able people. Think of yourself as a person who is making the global decisions and does not have time with petty work that can be done by someone less able than yourself. Don't get bogged down with trivia.

Stand apart: Meditate through PSI. Think about your goals and your aims and don't allow yourself to be sidetracked by less important and time consuming matters.

Don't accept negatives: Never take 'No' for an answer. If one route is blocked to you, find another route. If a person will not speak to you on the telephone, try and discover why and get to that person by other means. If you meet with a 'No' by a junior executive, jump rank. Don't be frightened to go straight to the top.

Communication: One of the most important assets in business. Read the chapter on communication again and follow the principles carefully. Learn to assess your business colleagues, partners and friends as well as the opposition. Understand body language and remember the all-important point about listening to other people.

Don't commit yourself: Don't say something you will afterwards regret or be unable to perform. You can still appear positive without committing yourself. Stand back and listen to others. Let them commit themselves. Don't offer suggestions gratuitously. Someone may shoot you down in flames. If uncertain of your facts, stay silent, otherwise you will provide ammunition for others to fire at you.

War games: Treat your business like a game. Don't get pent-up or emotional, that only brings stress. Play to win but enjoy the game. Act as much as you like, providing it brings you to the top but don't get emotionally entangled. If you do your judgment will suffer.

Changing course: Be adaptable but don't let the opposition see you change course mid-stream. Don't be indecisive. If you have made a statement, don't back down. Keep to your guns. Indecision does not inspire confidence.

Understand your target: Paint a PSI portrait of your target. If you are trying to impress your target, find out if he or she is conservative in tastes. Wear clothes that will be in keeping with the target's expectations. Discover the strengths and weaknesses of your target. Psych yourself to think like your target and play a role reversal game before the actual meeting.

Instinct: Allow your instincts to play a big part in your decision making when it is not possible to have all the facts. If you feel it is necessary to jump on an aeroplane to meet someone although it might be easier to call them by telephone later, then follow your instinct.   Opportunities do not present themselves for very long. A face to face meeting is far more effective than the telephone.

Timing: Perfect your timing techniques. Do not put a proposition or deal or try to sell anything at the wrong time. Be patient! Learn to wait for the appropriate moment. 'Read' the other person to establish the right moment for suggesting your proposal. If you feel it is better to go away, then do so. You can always come back whereas a rejection will make it far more difficult.

Risk: Be prepared to take calculated risks. A faint heart never wins the high stakes. If you know the person you want to get will be flying on Concorde, book a seat near him. What's a few thousand dollars when hundreds of thousands are at risk? The odds are that the person you want to see will be far more relaxed and open to suggestion on the aeroplane than when they are surrounded by staff and secretaries in an office. Even so, don't be carelessly over-optimistic and allow yourself to be duped. Unfortunately there are always sharks ready to prey on the financially unworldly. Thoroughly investigate before you commit funds and ask: what are other participants putting into it? Also, what do you *really* know about them and their track record? If all this sounds cautious, it is meant to. But when you have made your checks, you are satisfied and you 'feel' the venture is right for you, then take a calculated risk. If you are determined to succeed, you will.

Investment: Assume your venture is succeeding. Money is coming in. Then don't put all your eggs in one basket. Invest with security and spread your investments. Avoid the lure of remarkably high-interest financial offers. You may make an extra few per cent. But you MAY lose your money. And remember my view – there is nothing as sound as property investment. And the key is always to go for property in the best location. Why, in 1987 an estate agent sold a room *about the size of a large cupboard* a few doors from Harrod's store in London's Knightsbridge. The price: £36,000, equivalent to the cost of a modest house in an unfashionable provincial town!

Being noticed: Learn to stand out from other people. You can do this with your body language – dressing immaculately – by the way you communicate and with your presentations. Make people sit up and take notice. Be innovative and daring. Show people you are a leader and not a follower.

Go to the top: Save time and go straight to the top. Whether it's advice you are seeking or selling your goods, go straight to the top person. If he or she is the decision-maker, you are wasting your time convincing people down the line. Don't be afraid of paying top money for the best advice. It can save you much more money at the end of the day.

Combine your strengths: If someone else has better expertise than you, combine forces. Share your business with people who can benefit you. Without them you may never win the contract. Together you will have greater strength. Find an exciting partner with whom you can bounce ideas off each other. It can be a lot more profitable and more fun too.

Negotiation skills: Teach yourself negotiation skills. Much of these are to do with communication and timing and experience. List your ideas before you begin and practise what you are going to say. Read the other party and play role reversals. Get your timing absolutely right. Learn when not to speak. Argue from a position of strength. Work out beforehand exactly what financial concessions you will be willing to give or take.

Person management: Get your colleagues on your side. If you have employees, make them feel important and wanted. Give them incentives. Make them feel they are contributing to your success. Encourage them to be independent thinkers. Make them feel you care. Enthuse them with your ideas and vision.

Be lucky: I believe everyone makes their own good luck. I often hear people say of others that they were in the right place at the right time. A lot of their opponents could have been there too but were not. Luck can play a part but most often it is your PSI power at work. Positive thinking, perseverance, hard work and creating the opportunity that brings the reward which others mistake for luck.

I would also like to stress here that one of the ways to enjoy your success is to sleep with an easy conscience. Don't do anything illegal, or anything that may bring you into disrepute or damage your reputation. If you have a company which earns good money don't try and avoid taxes through illegal ways. Even some legal schemes for tax avoidance can be so complicated and time consuming that they could work against you in the end. Enjoy your success without being too greedy!

Show business PSI-force and the stars

Among my critics are those who say I should be using my powers only in a laboratory context and not on stage. My answer to that is very straightforward and honest. I am a performer and I believe in communicating my powers to the widest possible audience. Why should I just share it with a few grey-haired boffins tucked away in a dingy whitewashed room on a university campus when there are millions who enjoy sharing it with me? If my powers had not sparked the public's imagination, if they had not displayed the scope and possibilities those powers offered, then the boffins would never have bothered to research and examine them in the first place. Without my public appearances it is doubtful that Arthur Koestler would have left his money to create a chair in Parapsychology at Edinburgh University, the first professorial appointment on this subject in Britain!

A Shakespearian actor or actress who decides to become a soap star also has to suffer at the hands of critics who snootily consider that they should not be 'cheapening' themselves. But is giving greater pleasure to a wider audience cheapening oneself? To hold that view is to be elitist and selfish at the same time. Why should a few people impose their view on a majority and consider their personal pleasure to be above that of their fellow man? An actor is a communicator, and a successful communicator should be able to bridge the gap between light entertainment and serious works.

Showmanship is an exciting part of the public face of PSI. Communication takes part at every level. Body language, movement, speech, role playing, and image projection. Perhaps it is because of their continuous interaction with the inner self and an examination of mental processes to psych themselves for the different parts they play, that many actors are imbued with a natural sense of PSI. Some have even let their PSI projection get out of control. I know of at least several famous actors who have taken their projected personality so seriously that they have developed a serious identity problem.

Those people who have the natural gift for showmanship or acting, which after all is a highly developed PSI sense, have a tremendous weapon. Wisely used, it can make them immensely rich and famous. Don't think that you have to be the outgoing extrovert type to acquire this PSI skill. Although show business people are normally associated with having this characteristic, there are almost as many who are quite timid and reserved souls in spite of their power to effectively communicate and project on stage or on the screen.

Aaron Spelling would go unnoticed on a crowded train. As it is, the chances of seeing him on a train would be remote. He'd probably buy it before travelling on it. He looks a little frail, a little sad, almost self-effacing. Only by exchanging eye contact would you get a hint of this man's mountainous PSI power. He is a show business mogul of unimaginable proportions. He is America's Mr Television and the most successful independent TV film producer in the world. He is the king of Hollywood.

How did PSI-FORCE help him to the pinnacle of

showbiz success? I'll tell you. He was the fourth son of a Russian immigrant tailor and was raised in the ghetto in Dallas, Texas. His mother was a seamstress. As a child, Aaron was sickly and weak — the type of kid who had sand kicked in his face. Stronger children picked on him. He was beaten and abused, kicked and taunted. When he was only seven he had a nervous breakdown and stayed in bed for two years rather than be bullied. 'I could not face the bigger kids. I was their punching bag and they beat me up every day and called me "Jew Baby". I used my will power to end the assault. I willed my legs not to walk and stayed in bed for two years.'

His parents were poor. 'My brothers and I slept in the same bed feet to face. We were told it was fun to sleep that way and I grew up thinking that was how everyone slept. When I was fourteen I got a job carrying heavy flour sacks. They weighed more than me. I was paid a dollar fifty and gave half to my mother. Our clothes were hand-me-downs. My first suit was given to me by the US Army. I knew I could not go on in this way. I swore to myself that I would be wealthy and successful. It meant more to me than anything else.'

By the time Aaron came to Hollywood, he had had a close brush with death, sharpening his PSI senses even more. It happened while he was in the service. He was taken off a plane just two minutes before it became airborne. It crashed in Ohio killing everyone on board. Hollywood gave him film parts but they were not what he wanted. His main role he said was playing 'a deviate.' His life changed when he swapped roles and became a script writer and producer. He knew what he wanted which was to make money from series. He chose his goal and went for it.

He is acclaimed in the Guinness Book of World

Records for having produced more than 2000 hours of television. Nearly all his shows have been phenomenal successes. Among them: *Charlie's Angels, Dynasty, T J Hooker, Hart to Hart, Fantasy Island, Starsky and Hutch,* and *Vegas.*

With his bank balance mounting by the minute, billionaire Aaron still spends his money wisely. All his investments are rock solid. Like the flawless forty carat diamond he bought his beautiful wife Candy. It belonged to the late Shah of Persia and is one of the most sought after jewels in the world. Then the Spellings paid more than ten million dollars cash for Bing Crosby's old home, only to knock it down and rebuild it.

But old habits die hard. If Aaron is upset, he will stay in bed and he is often fearful his empire will collapse overnight. The buyers of his TV series think otherwise; he is guaranteed huge amounts for his new shows. Aaron's positive PSI towers over his more natural negativism. He has psyched himself to be successful. When he first submitted his own scripts he was knocked back for three years. But he kept going.

Curiously, while Aaron was building his empire on one side of the Atlantic, his counterpart, and later friend, Sir Lew Grade, was building his empire across the water in Britain. Both were from similar backgrounds although they had quite different temperaments.

Cigar-chomping tycoon Sir Lew Grade fled Russia with his family in 1912. He was one of three brothers, all of whom acquired fame and fortune. Life in London's East End was tough for the boys. Lew left school when he was fourteen and for a time helped his father Isaac in his clothing business. His life changed when he won first prize in a Charleston competition and became a professional dancer. With his tremendous energy and positive PSI power, Lew realised he would have to branch out into different forms of show business if he were to be really successful. He became an agent, getting up at five o'clock and working till late in the evening, a habit he continued throughout his career. While an agent, he helped a struggling television company to the road of success and never looked back. He took control of ATV and became the most important figure in commercial television in Britain.

Like Spelling, he knew instinctively what an audience wanted and gave it to them. He also wanted to be top at anything he did and his positiveness and super-sense of PSI was an invaluable asset. Like many other successful people, Sir Lew – who went on to become a Baron, Lord Grade – never looked back on mistakes. He did not want *post mortems* or regrets. Even when adding figures, he was the eternal optimist. Asked what two and two made, his reply was: 'Are you buying or selling?'

As with all great salesmen and artists, he is imbued with a PSI sense of fun and drama. His 'victims' have said of him: 'His repertoire was as varied as a cinema organist's and he could pull out all the stops – sentimental, threatening, pleading, admiring. His best act was when he would go down on his knees and fling out his arms, one hand still gripping the cigar.'

You don't have to be as rich and successful as Aaron Spelling or Sir Lew Grade to be happy, but perhaps you can learn something from the way these men live their lives and the motives behind their success. How motivated are you towards being a show business star or an entertainer?

Try this quiz answering each of the questions with either 'Yes,' 'Not sure,' or 'No.'

1. Do you like asking people challenging questions?
2. Are you always interested in how people react to what you do?
3. Do you often tell people about strange experiences you have had?
4. Are you guilty of sometimes using words people won't know the meaning of?
5. Do you tend to boast when in company?
6. Do you tend to dress to make people notice you?
7. Do you enjoy being the centre of attention?
8. Are you always trying to make people laugh?
9. Do you always dress up when going out or entertaining?
10. Is your voice loud and clear when talking in a group?
11. Do you enjoy trying to entertain people at parties?
12. Do you often find you are talking about yourself to others?
13. Do you often study your appearance in a mirror?
14. Are you never happier than when people compliment you?
15. Is what others think of you very important?

Scoring: Give yourself two points for every 'Yes' answer, one point for 'Not sure' and 0 points for 'No.' Now add your scores.

If you scored 11 or more points, then you may be the show business type of person. You enjoy saying clever and witty things and you tend to dress in order for others to notice you. You like being the centre of attention.

A score of less than 11 does not mean you will not

make it in show business. You could be an Aaron Spelling, a little insecure with others but still having fantastic PSI ability to communicate your way to stardom. Under 11 scorers could try living out their fantasies of stardom by writing TV scripts or plays. Try it! You might find you have an undiscovered genius for it.

PSI your way to stardom

Acting is a tough competitive business. You have to have your wits about you at all times, no matter how talented you might be. Read the chapter on communication again and again. You have to learn all the ways of communicating effectively. Use your PSI power to meditate and plan your roles. Use the mirror often to look at yourself. Speak to yourself. Reverse roles. Make yourself the audience.

You must also have the PSI positive approach to audiences. Even if you are a very private person, psych yourself that it is not you on stage but someone else. You are in someone else's shoes. You are in their minds. You are not revealing yourself to the audience but you are revealing the other person so it does not matter to you.

If you have a lesser role than someone else, tell yourself that you will stand out more with your presence. You can be the star and people will want to see you and hear your performance. Give them a shot of your electrical PSI personality that will rivet their attention in your direction. Go on stage as if *you* are the star and nobody else.

If you are doing a TV show, play to the camera for all you are worth. Imagine that the camera pointing at you is a viewing audience. Look at their faces in your mind and tell the camera that you are the best actor. Its attention on you must be undivided. You are captivating the audience with your presence. There is an aura about you which people want to see.

I have a lot of friends in show business with whom I have discussed the question of what gives some people star quality. Acting and actors are no longer limited to the stage. There are many people in politics who are actors and who could have been successful stars. Some do it the other way round and are actors first and later become politicians, like President Reagan. Others are content to use the House of Commons or Congress as their stage. There are many people in the legal and business professions who are also 'full-time actors.'

They have in common a need to communicate, a need to address audiences and a need to be seen on a stage. How well they achieve this need depends largely on their positive attitude through training, and through development of their PSI skills of communication. They must also have an almost intuitive feel for their audience so that they can come across sympathetically.

British Prime Ministers have had an excellent record for their stage performance. The veteran Tory 'Supermac', Harold MacMillan, when on lecture tours to America, was famed for his 'reading' of his audiences. He knew just the moment when to tell his aides to laugh or to cry at a particular point in his speech.

The former Labour PM Harold Wilson was such a good actor that he has been asked to personally appear as himself in various productions. He is also extremely popular on the American lecture circuit and his delivery is impeccable. When talking privately over a glass with friends in the House of Lords, people are spellbound by his conversation.

I believe too that Mrs Thatcher should be issued

with an Equity card for her very fine performances. She is a polished and accomplished actress and delivers her well-rehearsed lines with aplomb. Through her PSI powers, which are quite extraordinary, she has been able to tread a delicate path to stay in power despite a number of unpopular measures. The image she projects is one of total conviction and belief in her role as Prime Minister and as such, she inspires tremendous confidence.

President Reagan learnt all his tricks and PSI power many years ago while still an actor and was able to make a remarkably smooth transition to politics as a result. His powers to read people and appeal to them through positive PSI and the image he portrays of a humble, fun-loving, caring President has won over the populace. They like him even if they don't care much for his party machine.

The Russian leader Mikhail Gorbachev is so adaptable that he could fit into any political system and reach the top. He has a natural ability to respond to PSI feelings put out by others as well as being able to project his own effectively. His personal charm has not gone unnoticed in the western world and may even make him enemies among the Politburo in Russia. However, it is unlikely that he will suffer because of his in-built early warning radar (PSI) system.

Assassinated President John F. Kennedy was a classic example of a person helped by his family to reach the pinnacle of success. There was, and still is, tremendous PSI-FORCE in the Kennedy clan. They are all on the same wavelength and this gives them great positive mental power. Using this, they were able to push JFK to the Presidency in record time. He personally had an abundance of PSI power. He was able to project an honest and glamorous image and had the world eating out of the palm of his hand.

Using his personal appeal – a strong factor of PSI – his popularity grew and grew. Unfortunately, there was another extremely strong PSI drive that was natural to him and which he could not control: his sexual drive. It was so powerful that, had he not been shot, I believe he would have eventually lost the presidency through a sexual scandal.

Although he was a manipulator of mankind and made a tremendous impact on millions, this failing became too much of a threat to his position. He was on course for a collision with fate because of his sexuality but was tragically saved the dishonour by an assassin's bullet. Had he been an actor, he would have been more famous than Robert Redford.

It was inevitable that he became mixed up with a woman whose sexual PSI was as strong as his. That woman was Marilyn Monroe, the most desirable woman in the world who will be remembered for ever, not as Jack Kennedy's mistress, but for her own powerful sexuality. She died on 5 August, 1962 from an overdose. She was thirty-six years old, and there were men who would have moved mountains for her.

Her PSI ability to project sexuality was legendary. She was able to do it enticingly but in taste. Yet she wasn't the prettiest woman in the world. But she knew when to trigger her sexual PSI and capture the hearts of powerful men. Among her many lovers was the president's own brother, Senator Bobby Kennedy, who was also assassinated.

JFK knew how to win the heart of the nation but Marilyn could manipulate him. She could look into a man's eyes and immediately know what was wanted of her. With men like the Kennedys, she gave them all she had. Her PSI sexuality captivated the passion and desire for her in most men. She played PSI games with men. From the sparkle in her eyes, the movement of her mouth, down to her wiggle, she told men she was all woman and those powerful enough would be allowed to have her.

In the end she overdid it and the same power took its revenge. It boomeranged back on her in a most devastating way. She died as she had come into the world. Naked and alone.

John Lennon, who became very friendly with me, kept his appointment with fate: Death. He was fascinated by PSI and wanted to experience every conceivable aspect of the natural and supernatural. He was a walking PSI powerhouse. He wanted to transcend all that was ordinary and mundane and enter a different world of boundless possibilities and new experiences. He believed in out of body experiences, in drugs that released inhibitions of space and reality and went beyond the sixth sense. He tried to use his PSI powers way beyond that of a performer and song writer. He wanted to reach another dimension and get from that 'wondrous place' a new meaning to the lyrics and music he would write.

He also had someone very special in his wife, Yoko Ono. He was enveloped in her. He lived inside her soul, and she in his. She is almost as psychic as John and reminds me of a white witch. She knew how to return his PSI love and was able to direct him and give him the pleasures he needed from life. But most of all they had *love*. John was almost drunk on it. It was a spiritual union the like of which I had never before seen.

John was interested in my philosophy and wanted me to expound on extra-terrestrial connections. He wanted to hear about another life, as though he was soon going to enter it. I think he knew something was going to happen. In my mind he was ready for some kind of transition. That happened on the day he was shot. He was then transformed into something else that he wanted to be and arrived at another place, another dimension.

The sad thing about John was his dependence on drugs which he took to escape from normality. He had tasted LSD and believed that he could find a world similar to the one he had experienced while in a hallucinatory state. That was a world with no horizons, of green trees, rainbow flowers, sweet smelling air and purifying melodies. He did not want reality. He did not want to lose this 'paradise' state.

Elvis Presley might have appeared a simple uncomplicated man on the outside but his inner self was a mass of contradictions. He was an unhappy man whose PSI powers rebelled against him in the end because he had abused his body so badly. At his peak, he was a magical entertainer who controlled his PSI talents and sent his audiences wild with animal vibrations and body language. His telepathy was astute enough to pick out exactly what the crowds wanted and he gave it to them. He had a low sexual PSI and would rather drive a white Cadillac than have sex with a woman. I believe he was in contact with his dead twin brother and this also brought him much unhappiness.

Humphrey Bogart was a master illusionist. He was able to project an image which people wanted to see rather than a real image of himself which was not very physically attractive. Yet women were beating a path to his door because of the strong sexual vibes emanating from this man. No one can quite explain the phenomenon that produced this legend but I think the reason for his success was that through his PSI powers, he captured a dream and then gave it to the man and woman in the street.

The PSI power of Grace Kelly was attached to her beauty, voice, dress and aristocratic bearing. She already possessed a regal quality before she became a princess. She knew instinctively how to bridge the gap between reality and fantasy which drove men wild. She had the innocent beauty which captivated a prince's heart. She knew she would achieve a dream, a fairytale come true. Even when she was a real life princess, her PSI power helped her carry out her duties with distinction and honour, as if she was born to the task.

My PSI portrait of Robert Redford is of a very private man who uses his PSI abilities to seduce and communicate with the camera. He has an uncanny ability to project his irresistible powers and give himself an ordinary appeal, like that of the fresh good-looking boy next door, but with a god-like quality. He uses his looks to great advantage. He is very handsome and charismatic and induces people, especially women, to have a deep craving for him.

The phenomenal success of Harrison Ford is, in my opinion, a direct result of his PSI powers which he uses to project simplicity and the image of the robust all-American male. Harrison might be an adventurer but he makes it look easy enough for people to imagine that they could do it themselves. He mesmerises women with his tough but tender approach. His voice employs PSI to give it added appeal and he is in full control when acting, unlike many in his profession who have to do exactly as instructed by the film director; he will not bow to a director. He is a natural and can absorb the energies of people around him, thus multiplying his own powers in the process. Paul Newman is very much in the same mould but more subdued. Bruce Springsteen, the singer, has also been endowed with a similar gift which he uses magically on stage.

Bob Geldof has the power to be a very fine politi-
cian if only he had a good shave and cleaned up his
image. He is a political activist, a man who uses his
powers through songs and lyrics to effect changes in
the world. He is an interesting PSI subject. Bob came
from a humble Dublin background and started as a
lead singer with his own group, The Boomtown
Rats. He gathered together his PSI powers and then
faced the world looking like a bum: unshaven and
ungroomed. Yet the world has accepted him as an
honest person trying to help others. What a clever
use of PSI to bring yourself to the world as you are.
As a result, big business and popular musicians have
followed this man to his crucial goal: saving
children in Africa. His powers worked miracles in
reaching the hearts of the western world and then
opening their purses.

Forever inseparable from her magical performance
as *Funny Girl*, Barbra Streisand is one of the richest
self-made women in the world, thanks to her positive PSI approach. She is a lady who used her powers
for the *one* goal. She wanted to make it big – really
big. And she's there. She only had voice and
charisma to start with and lots of positive feelings.
With her mind, she manipulated her way to stardom
which she then achieved through her voice. When
she sings there is a PSI energy detectable by me in
every note; it penetrates my senses. Her music
transforms the atmosphere to a higher plane. She is
also a natural actress. She came from a poor family
and despite her success, has the ability to be herself.
She knows what it is like to be on the breadline. She
also has enough PSI nous to preserve her wealth!

I rubbed shoulders with John Wayne once in the
Beverly Wilshire hotel, Los Angeles. Outside the
hotel, a row of little old American ladies, many with

blue-rinsed hair and rose-painted faces, waited for him to emerge. As John and I walked out together, one old dear grabbed me and asked: 'Is that him? John Wayne? . . . isn't he beautiful! He's my all-American boy!' That summed up the impression he gave me: a tremendous PSI strength with positive attributes, the hero, the macho American. Wayne knew how to project good in such a way that anything less than good became positively bad. His was the PSI projection of idealism. Even though he was then in his 60s, each of those ladies thought of him as a son.

Omar Sharif talks with his eyes. His Middle-East background gives him an air of mystery and excitement. He has a very definitive aura and many women find him absolutely irresistible. He uses his PSI power when playing bridge or when he is gambling. His eyes are piercing and exotic, a perfect complement to his handsome facial features.

Raquel Welch: here is the classic example of a wife who made good with PSI. She may never have been an 'ordinary' home-body in fact, but to see her in the street you would think she was a perfectly ordinary but attractive mother who stays at home minding the children. Her PSI power changed this by concentrating her energies and talents on becoming a sex symbol. It is difficult to change your personality but she managed it. She is also a master of illusion: in my mind I had an image of an Amazon, but when I saw her in real life I was surprised at how small she actually is.

What a remarkable use of PSI powers Michael Jackson has! He uses it to make his body move in extraordinary ways and to write and sing songs and hit the audiences with them at just the right time. I am worried in case he has exhausted these powers.

Since he has been so groomed and polished from birth, he must be careful not to abuse the natural gifts he has. PSI power has also given him the facility to appeal equally to both men and women.

From a very young age, the brilliant film maker Steven Spielberg learned all about PSI and other dimensions. He liked it so much that he wanted to continue to be part child forever, although his artistic talent has grown up. As a child, he is a little introverted in adult company but can change his image to that of a romantic adventurer. He has translated his fantasies to the screen and has a superb sense of timing as well as being a cinematic sponge, absorbing the public taste and then serving it back to them on a delicious plate. Each of his films made a minimum of two hundred million dollars and his blockbusters – *E.T.*, *Raiders of the Lost Ark*, *Jaws*, and *Close Encounters Of The Third Kind* – made a total of three billion dollars!

In her youth, Joan Collins never used her powers and it is just lately that she has realised the true force existing within her. By using her PSI powers as a negative influence in her TV roles, she overcame her own previous 'failures' and became a roaring success. She knows just how to carry herself, how to dress and what to say and eat and who to date for maximum impact. I feel that she is a great believer in astrology and that she is an avid reader of astrological signs. She is a lady who will follow their lead and allow her superstitions and feelings to influence her career. She would have been very good as a company director or as a lawyer and displays strong intuitive powers.

Elton John writes and sings about hidden parts of his inner self. His PSI powers are down to earth. A part of him wants to be free and explicit but because of social pressures, he cannot do exactly as he feels. I feel he is living in a world of fantasy and pretence in an effort to cover up these inner PSI feelings. His music is brilliant and reaches out dramatically to the man in the street. When he touches the keys of a piano they respond as if to a supernatural command. But music apart, I feel he has many minuses and PSI complexes which have come about as a result of not having 'found' his true self.

Johnny Carson: He is amazingly successful, with a façade to his nature which belies the true man underneath. He resists the supernatural yet I believe he has a great power there which, without him admitting to it, has helped him become successful as a TV interviewer and multi-millionaire. He is a very hard but clever man who surrounds himself with good advisers. His many influential friends can open almost any door he needs opened and I suspect he would take full advantage of any situation that could further his career. Underneath however, I suspect he is an unhappy man, although he has found a beautiful companion in Alexis Maas, which has made his unhappiness a little easier to bear. Deep inside, he knows he is a complex man with many minuses to his character. That is why his façade is so cold. I think I am right in believing that he was once an amateur magician. Although he wants to dig deeply into the subjects he interviews, he does not like being interviewed himself and considers his own privacy sacrosanct.

So strong are the inquisitory powers of David Frost that he should perhaps have been born in another period – The Spanish Inquisition? David has an aura and sense of PSI that I have never before seen in any TV interviewer. He also has the intellect to match. PSI techniques have shown him to be charming at the beginning, courteous throughout, and then unexpectedly strike at his victim who does not know what has happened until he or she leaves the chair. This talent has allowed him to interview 'impossible' subjects like Richard Nixon and Henry Kissinger who would refuse lesser interviewers but rise to the challenge of Frost. His energy has made him a successful businessman in tandem with his TV personality image.

Terry Wogan has PSI sensibility. He comes across as the easy-going friendly TV chat-show host but underneath is a shrewd brain and a startlingly successful businessman. Let no one underestimate his intellect. He is bristling with PSI power even when everyone else thinks he is bumbling on in his merry careless way. There are few more polished performers than he on British television today.

Derek Jameson: I am inspired by this man who, like the phoenix, rose from the ashes and has continued rising. Derek has edited more Fleet Street newspapers than most other editors. At a mature stage of his life he sued the giant British Broadcasting Corporation and lost nearly every penny he ever made. But so strong was his positive PSI power that he fought back to become one of the most successful early morning radio announcers on – wait for it – British Broadcasting Corporation radio! That takes some PSI power! I believe he has a very strong sense of the supernatural, but coupled to that is a down-to-earth personality, reflected in his London cockney accent which some mornings is accompanied by a strange gargling sound like a voice trapped down a plug hole.

Never, but never underestimate the powerhouse in the mind of Barbara Cartland. This lady is larger than life. Her PSI shines out like a beacon. No matter what you think of her, you probably will never really know or understand what goes on inside her mind. At over eighty years of age, she is dictating books, designing interiors of expensive flats, commenting on health and beauty and running a large and beautiful household. Her positive PSI is without question the strongest I have ever seen. She has been willing to tackle almost any subject with a vigour and energy that would have long submerged others. She was the closest friend of Prince Charles' uncle, Louis Mountbatten, and is the mother of Raine Spencer who is married to Princess Di's father.

Barbara manages, virtually single-handedly, a multi-national enterprise with the directness and ruthlessness of a top flight chief executive. Yet at the same time, this supreme romance writer, is an outrageously flamboyant dresser and a frank, open and confident woman who says what she thinks. Her PSI-FORCE will live forever.

Health and happiness through PSI power

I never cease to be amazed by the smug attitude of people who feel 'safe' because they have paid for an expensive health insurance package. They are convinced that by doing so they will not have to worry about their health because all expenses will be paid when they go to hospital. That could be a fatal mistake. The best and least expensive insurance against hospitalisation is to take care of your body. It's free. Lead a healthy life and don't abuse your body. If you do that, it is most likely you won't need to have that expensive cure. I am not saying that you should cancel your insurance policies forthwith. If it makes you secure, then by all means get insurance in case of accidents or tragic illnesses over which you have no control, but do not neglect your body as a result.

Did you know that two of the most common reasons for seeing your local doctor are respiratory symptons (coughs and colds) and nervous system disorders (emotional problems)? And both of these can be treated by *you*. By using your PSI power you can get rid of problems before they develop into more complicated and severe forms of illness. Of course, if they *do* persist, you will want to see your doctor, even if it is just for some reassurance.

I am a strong believer in holistic medicine, which involves doctors being open-minded in their healing approach and treating the patient as a whole rather than just treating the disease or a particular part of the body. Throughout the world more and more doctors are coming round to holistic practice.

If, for example, a patient goes to the doctor complaining of frequent headaches or migraine, he or she might be given strong medicine to relieve the pain. By doing this, the doctor will have treated the symptom rather than the cause, which could be due to emotional stress. The holistic approach would involve inquiring into the patient's mental and physical state in general. The doctor would find out if the patient was suffering from stress or strain at work or in a domestic situation. The treatment might then involve not giving the patient any painkilling drugs at all, but would rather teach the patient how to relax mentally and do away with anxiety and stress. The migraine would then hopefully be cured without the need for drugs.

How healthy are you? Try the health quiz answering each question with either 'Yes,' 'Not sure,' or 'No.'

1. Do you rarely feel tense or restless?
2. Are you the opposite of the anxious type?
3. Do you have a varied and well-balanced diet?
4. Are you in favour of health foods?
5. Do you aim to walk at least a mile a day?
6. Do you still participate in sport?
7. Are you the relaxed, easy-going type?
8. Do you find it easy to get to sleep at night?
9. Is your weight about right for your height?
10. Do you actively avoid too much fat and sugar in your diet?
11. Do you experience a sense of well-being after vigorous exercise?
12. Do you get a sort of sensuous pleasure from physical activity?

13. Do you enjoy action-packed holidays?
14. Do you feel fresh and energetic in the mornings?
15. Do you feel younger than your years?

Scoring: Give yourself 2 points for each 'Yes' answer, 1 point for 'Not sure' and 0 points for 'No.'

A score of 16 or more means you are health conscious and care about your body. With this attitude, you should be in reasonable health at least. The components of general health are being relaxed, well-nourished but not over-weight, and active. A score of 22 or more means you are striving for real physical fitness and health and the chances are you will rarely have to see a doctor. You are also a good PSI candidate!

A score of 15 or less could mean that either you are one of those lucky people who is naturally healthy without having to do much exercise, or that you ought to start thinking more about your physical condition. If the latter applies, consult a doctor and ask for help with diet and exercise.

One finding from psychic research is that PSI ability is related to a relaxed state. Other things being equal, a tranquil person has a better chance of discovering psychic powers.

Believing as I do in the power of the mind over matter and mind over body, I am convinced that there are many cures we can achieve ourselves where conventional medicine might not be of use or where only the symptom is treated, not the cause. A good doctor will be aware of the positive powers of healing that are within each and every one of us and if you are worried about your health you should always consult your general practitioner first.

Getting the best out of your doctor

Use your PSI knowledge of communication to talk to your GP. Don't put your doctor on a pedestal and then be afraid to ask questions or tell him or her of your inner fears. Remember your GP's purpose in being there is to help *you*. But you will get more out of your doctor if your approach also takes into account the pressures and needs of your GP. Doctors in Britain are often over-worked and sometimes underpaid, whereas doctors in America are often overpaid and sometimes under-worked. So you should be aware of your GP's status when making your approach.

In a busy surgery, a doctor will tend to rush through a long list of patients devoting just a few moments to each one. If you feel you need more time to explain your problems, don't allow yourself to be ushered out of the surgery and then feel as though you have been ignored. This will only worsen your condition and possibly make you depressed. Before seeing the doctor, plan your approach. Work out what you want to say and what you see as your medical problem and what you might consider are the reasons for your illness. Note everything down on a piece of paper so you don't forget. A considered explanation by a patient will immediately inform the doctor that you are a serious person with a proper complaint and there is a need for him or her to listen to you and to help you. Your status will be elevated immediately because you will not be considered a time-waster.

Tell your doctor: 'I know you are a very busy person and I don't want to take up more of your time than is necessary. I have thought about my illness and have listed my symptoms and what I consider to be the problem. Do you think you can help me?' Be polite and pleasant to the doctor; make your GP like you and want to help you. By stating your case to the doctor as I have suggested, you have also offered a challenge which will be more interesting to the doctor than writing another prescription for a run of the mill complaint. So make the doctor react to your positive PSI. Establish a good rapport. Treat your doctor as an equal. Establish eye contact and charm the doctor into liking you and make him or her want to help you. Don't be a time-waster; you will get very little sympathy and not much help. Your future prospects with that doctor might also suffer if he associates you in this category of patients. Don't telephone your GP with minor complaints which you can effectively deal with yourself.

Doctors cannot always tell what is wrong with a patient. You have a right to ask the doctor if he or she can tell you what the prognosis might be, but don't expect your GP to always be right or to know! An honest doctor will admit failure to diagnose. If that happens you should either request referral to a specialist or try another doctor or an alternative cure. But when it is said that you are seriously ill and need an operation, I still recommend getting two or three opinions. The first diagnosis is not *always* right. For example, lots of women have undergone hyster-ectomies when they have not been necessary.

If you or members of your family are to have an operation in a hospital and you are concerned about it, you have a right to talk to the consultant or the registrar about your anxiety. Ask the consultant who will be performing the operation. If you are having the operation in a general hospital under the national health scheme, there is a good chance that the operation will be carried out by an inexperienced

176

doctor learning his craft. The registrar might try to relieve your concern by saying that the young doctor will be supervised by the consultant and that you need not worry. If that assurance does not satisfy you, tell the registrar that you are not happy about a trainee surgeon performing the operation and give the reasons for your concern. It is your body and you have a right to be concerned. A consultant might be too busy to pay too much attention to a particular operation in a large teaching hospital and mistakes are made. Be firm and be positive. You have a right to be anxious about this. Unless you establish a personal relationship with the surgeon or consultant, your body is just another 'job lot' on the operating table and there is no need for the doctor to treat it differently. If however you have communicated to the consultant that you are concerned about your body and you want to ensure every care is taken at the operation, the 'job lot' will become more meaningful and the results may be more beneficial.

I try to avoid doctors where possible because I believe positive PSI to be an effective healer. I know of many cases where doctors have been unable to account for a cure in patients who have suffered terrible afflictions, including cancer. I have met a number of famous men and women who have shown me scars from earlier operations for cancer. They have told me how doctors gave them a limited time to live and twenty years or so later they were still talking to me about it. Some had changed their attitude to nutrition, and all of them had changed their mental attitudes. They had fought off the cancer with positive inner strength, either in groups or singly. Some even went on to make fortunes writing about their cures.

Look back on your life and think about all the people you have known. Look back at your own medical history. Have you always succumbed to colds and flu? Have you been able to beat diseases? Have any of your friends? Has anyone you know made a miraculous recovery? I'm sure every one of us will be able to find examples of unexplained or 'miracle' cures.

I do not consider such cures to be miracles. I accept them for what they are: MIND OVER BODY CONTROL. My very good friend, the classical pianist and composer Byron Janis, who lives with his wife Maria in New York, absolutely depends on his hands for his living. As a distinguished pianist he has been asked to play at the White House and has performed for Presidents Reagan and Carter. He was also the first American pianist to go to Moscow on a cultural exchange basis. His wife Maria is the daughter of the famous actor Gary Cooper.

Byron confided in me a long time ago that his hands suffered from arthritis. He had kept this a secret from the world for many years. I felt so sorry for him. Firstly he had been such a good friend to me; when I first arrived in New York he had lent me forty thousand dollars to set up home, and secondly, I was deeply worried that a brilliant musical talent and career could be threatened by a cruel twist of fate. 'Byron,' I said. 'Let's work this out; you and me together. Let's fight this crippling arthritis with our minds. Make it go away. It will not affect you. You will not allow the arthritis to take over and stop your splendid career.'

It worked! Byron believes in PSI power and our combined effort has kept his arthritis under control for many years. If ever it threatens to return, Byron calls me from wherever he is performing and we both think positively and will it to go away. He has a tremendously strong faith in PSI and I act as a trigger to set off the positive anti-arthritis reactions in him.

The wife of an ambassador once cured herself after I had triggered positive thoughts in her mind. She had been suffering from arthritis and could not walk without help. While watching me perform on television with metal bending feats, she asked herself why, if I could bend spoons, could I not do something for her legs. The following morning she jumped out of bed and danced around her room. She was cured. Her positive PSI had succeeded in overcoming her negative bodily malfunctions. Mind over body!

And she is just one of countless people. In London there is a woman I know of who was suddenly stricken with a devastating cancer when she had two children just coming up to their teens and a loving but distraught husband. In hospital, the specialists recommended a major operation with a slender chance of saving her life. The woman, Gill, briefly accepted she would almost certainly die. Indeed, her own brother, a cancer specialist from Germany, was called in too. He agreed there was precious little hope. Then Gill thought of her son and of her daughter and of her husband. She determined: 'To hell with this. I will beat this. I will not die,' even as she lay immobile, in appalling pain and near to death. The result: Gill survived the operation. She went from strength to strength; all her lovely hair (lost during treatment) grew again and she returned, restored to her family. The surgeons and her brother marvelled. Gill's inner strength had triumphed.

As a young man I loved horror movies and always wanted to star in them as a Count Dracula figure. So when I had the chance to meet Christopher Lee, that famous horror movie actor, I was thrilled to bits. He was my hero. Recently he came to me and said he was about to have open-heart surgery and that he was frightened and quite depressed about it. I told him to switch in to PSI power and to be positive. 'Your operation will be successful and you will heal fast,' I said. 'Tell your mind that everything will go well. Your mind will have power over your body. Convince yourself you will have a successful operation.'

Christopher did just that. He concentrated very deeply before surgery and the operation was very successful. He called me afterwards to say it was a success. I then told him he would have to concentrate on the next stage – the post operative pain. I explained how the mind can control pain, or at the very least, diminish it. As a result, he suffered much less pain than he might have done. It worked really well and we've been good friends since.

I am sure I helped that very big star of movies and TV, Richard Chamberlain, overcome a bad bout of depression. I was in Hollywood at the time and Richard was very down. I told him all about the beneficial effects of PSI power and positive thinking.

Self diagnosis

You are by now familiar with the technique of looking at your real self. What I would like you to do now is for you to have a very candid look at your body. First of all, go through some relaxation exercises and meditate on your general health. Spend quite a lot of time relaxing and then tell yourself you are going to have an honest self-assessment of your physical and mental well-being. Now take off all your clothes and stand in front of the mirror. Do you see a healthy specimen? Or do you see something that is not right and you would like to change? Ask yourself the following questions:

My body:

1. Am I too fat or too thin?
2. Do my eyes look alert and healthy or are they tired-looking and lifeless?
3. Does my hair look healthy?
4. What is my skin like? Do I have an excess of pimples or rashes, could I improve my skin?
5. Does my body need toning up?
6. How do I normally stand? Am I too slouched or do I stand upright with my shoulders back and my body straight?
7. How do I hold my head?
8. Is the general impression I make to other people one which says I have a healthy body or not?
9. What is the general state of my nails and hair? Are my nails well manicured or not? Is my hair neat and well groomed?
10. Do I like what I see?

Make a note of all the things you like and don't like about your body. If you have scars or birth marks which cannot be helped do *not* note that down as a minus point. You must learn to live with those and not feel that they limit you in any way. Tell yourself that those marks will not affect you and that your personality and charm and your overall image will be wonderful.

Having noted all the improvements that are possible, tell yourself that from this moment you are going to improve the image you have just seen. Tell yourself that whatever it is that you don't like is not the real you. It is a temporary image and you will improve it in a very short time. Tell yourself that if you don't like what you see then others won't like it either. However, if you are perfectly happy with your body the way it is, even if it is too fat or your hair is too long, don't try and change it. It will not make any difference to your social acceptance because you have such a strong and positive PSI personality that your defects will not be noticed.

General Health:

1. Am I a person who is prone to stress and anxiety?
2. How often do I get anxious or stressed?
3. Do I get enough exercise?
4. What do I do when I experience stress?
5. Do I smoke too much?
6. Do I drink too much?
7. Do I eat good and nutritious food?
8. Do I eat slowly and relax over my meals or do I bolt down my food?
9. Do I get colds often?
10. Do I suffer from frequent headaches or migraine?
11. Am I irritable with my family or friends or at work?
12. Do I tend to raise my voice often or shout at people?
13. Do I get angry quickly?
14. Am I often bored for long periods of time?
15. Do I suffer from lack of concentration?
16. Am I forever waiting for something to happen in my life?
17. Do I have any recurring pains or feel unwell in any part of my body?
18. Do I get tired easily?
19. Do I worry about things before they happen?
20. Do I sleep soundly?

From the above list, note down all the negative aspects of your general health and the improvements that *you* can make. Be totally honest with yourself. *You* will know if any of the above problems apply and how badly affected you are by them. Don't wait to act. Do so right away. Now. Change your unhealthy ways from this very second. Be positive. Most of us have suffered from one or all of the harmful and negative aspects of health outlined in the above questions. Psych yourself to good health!

Emotional problems

Anxiety and stress can produce physical manifestations in our health which disguise their true cause. Often, *you* will be able to treat this yourself through positive thought and PSI power.

Sexual impotence is quite common in otherwise virile young men, if they have emotional problems due to anxiety. A woman may suffer from frigidity for the same reason though probably without the extra hangups experienced by males if they cannot perform the sexual act. Ask yourself why you think you have this problem. Is it through stress at work? Or through financial worries or family problems? Or is it because of feelings of guilt about the sexual act itself? Tell yourself that you will not allow it to affect you. Don't rush the sexual act. Learn to relax and enjoy your time with the other partner. By relaxing properly and emptying your mind of negative thoughts your problem will go away. Tell yourself that you are not alone in experiencing problems of this nature. Assure yourself it is a common ailment and will last only as long as you allow your worries to get you down.

A pain in the left side of the chest away from the

heart can come about as a result of stress and emotional worries. Alternatively, you may experience pain in your stomach just below the ribs. Anxiety causes your heart to work faster in preparation for danger. It may result in palpitations which you might mistake for something more serious, adding even more worry to your general state of anxiety. This in turn may lead to unpleasant conditions like constipation or nervous diarrhoea. Unless you have analysed your general health and understand the effect that stress is having on your life, you will not be in a position to cure the ailment and at best, your doctor will only treat the one-off symptom which is bound to recur.

Phobias and skin rashes can also be the symptoms of a nervous disorder or stress. Have you ever felt the world was closing in on you and you can't escape from it? That is a common phobia and should be tackled with relaxation and by telling yourself that your fears are without substance and your mind will not take any notice of them. Of course I have felt like this myself. And I have conquered it, too, by repeating steadily to myself 'Relax, Uri, relax', just as though I was hypnotising myself.

Don't be afraid to discuss your innermost fears. If you have any sexual hang-ups, or feel that you deviate from the sexual norm, then discuss your problem with suitable counsellors. By keeping your problems to yourself you will only make them worse and create further emotional upsets. A lot of medical problems are caused by men and women who are not confident of their own sexuality or have secret fears about whether they are homosexual. There is an added problem today and that is the horrendous problem of AIDS.

The PSI approach to AIDS

Sexual fears and anxieties have always plagued mankind and resulted in many different manifestations of illnesses. Those fears still exist today. They include fears of unwanted pregnancies, anxieties about masturbation and guilt about illicit sex. Those every day fears that we have accepted as part of the normal risk in human relationships now pale into insignificance with the scourge of AIDS. This is the most terrifying sexual disease known to man, threatening to create leper-type communities of its ever increasing victims. It fuels fears because of the way it creeps up on its unsuspecting victims. When you least expect it, the disease will suddenly affect you or a friend. Your fear may then be intensified, especially if your friend has been living with you or been in your company.

Like it or not, we are all going to have to live with AIDS until a cure or vaccine is found. A frightening aspect of the AIDS virus, which breaks down a body's resistance to disease, is that a large number of unfortunate victims are facing a back-dated sentence of death. The virus had already infected thousands of people some five to six years before we were made aware of this global menace.

As you read this, there are hundreds of thousands of people throughout the world who are at this very moment undergoing agonising periods of uncertainty and despair wondering if they are infected with the virus. Do not make the mistake of thinking this disease is entirely limited to homosexuals. Unhappily some bigoted people who have until now thought the disease was a kind of divine retribution against homosexuals may find innocent members of their own family suffering from AIDS. It is a disease that has infected normal heterosexuals, wives, husbands, daughters and sons and it will continue to do so with a vengeance. One reason it has been more prominent in homosexuals is because they tend to have many more partners than heterosexuals. So how can PSI power help?

Anxiety and AIDS: No matter what disease you have, a positive attitude of mind will help you fight it or come to terms with it. Psi power gives you the positive attitude to look for alternatives and make the best of good or bad situations. If you suspect you have AIDS or anyone close to you has AIDS, do not despair. You can carry the AIDS virus and still live a normal life. But you can infect someone else who could then die as a result of your selfishness or carelessness. I would recommend that you see your doctor and explain to him your fears about AIDS. A good many people will resist going to their doctors and make their condition worse through extreme anxiety which in itself could cause an onset of the more harmful aspects. I also think you owe it to your partner or friends and to yourself, to find out if you really have it or not. If after being tested for AIDS you are cleared, think of the relief! You can once more engage in normal happy and healthy activities rather than spend weeks and months agonising over your fears. But in future, take every care possible to guard against infections. Use a sheath or other protection if you are not fully sure of your partner.

If you find the test is positive and you do have AIDS, take stock of the situation. By being responsible you can avoid passing on the virus to friends. And there is a good chance anyway that the disease will not progress in your body. Psych yourself to resist its worst effects. Say to yourself that you know you are carrying the virus but that is all. It will remain in your body but it will not harm you. Say to yourself how responsible you are and have been regarding your friends and that life can still be good. You will receive a lot of mental comfort and self-respect by being responsible.

Non-victims: Hopefully you are among the vast majority who does not have AIDS. So, consider yourself and your family next time you have sex with a relative stranger. It is a sad state of affairs that in our progressive times, young people, whom western society no longer condemns for having loving relationships outside marriage, now face a horrifying gamble with fate if they are to proceed with a natural and enjoyable activity. That is why I stressed in an earlier chapter that your safest partner in a sexual relationship is your wife or husband, or the person you have lived with for a number of years. But what if they have been led astray?

My advice is to face the problem and communicate honestly with your partner or with the person with whom you are about to have a relationship. Explain your fears. He or she should feel the same way. Question your past, and if you are in any doubt at all, use a protective before you engage in sex. Is a brief moment of pleasure worth dying for? If you have any doubts about the other person, then be positive about refusing sex. If your inner self tells you that what you are about to do is reckless and stupid, stop yourself. Do not indulge in sex if you have any fears at all. Masturbation is a healthy alternative for both young and old.

AIDS – No escape: If the virus has started to affect you adversely there is little point in despairing. You will receive help from counsellors and friends. Be positive. Accept your lot. Look back on the happy memories of your life and see if you can lighten the load of those friends you love and have known for many years. They will be suffering too. Show them you are positive. Try and help others in the same situation as yourself. Remember that you are not alone and that you can still help and be happy in company. Research for a cure or partial cure is ceaseless. And please remember, miracles *do* happen.

Addictions

If you have an addiction, there could be a very simple reason for it and with professional help you might easily solve your problem. If, on the other hand, the issues are more complicated, you should try and fathom out the various factors at work. Do this through PSI contemplation and meditation. Ask yourself questions about your lifestyle and why you are abusing your body. In all cases you should also seek professional help.

Smoking: Beat this dangerous habit with love. Say to yourself: 'I am damaging the health of those people I love by making them breathe this deadly smoke. It is harming them and my own body. I will stop straight away.' Take out a white handkerchief and blow smoke into it and you will see how quickly it is discoloured. Ask yourself if it is wise to do that to your lungs. Psych yourself to conquer this addiction. Draw a monster every time you feel like a cigarette and kill it with anger. Instead of smoking, do exercises. Breathe in deeply and tell yourself how wonderful it is to have fresh air in your lungs.

Drugs: Drugs will destroy you. Even medically prescribed drugs are dangerous. Try and avoid all drugs. If you are hooked on narcotics, seek professional help and go to those people who love you. Tell them you are addicted and that you want to be helped. Psych yourself to resist the urge for more. Tell yourself they will kill you, that you are not enjoying them but living in a fool's paradise. Join self-help organisations and listen to the positive stories of people who have conquered their addiction.

Alcohol: An excess of this is just as dangerous as cigarettes and other drugs. Ask yourself why you are drinking to excess. Tell yourself that you are harming your body and that you could kill yourself and even other people around you. Stop drinking and relax and meditate. Discover the reasons for your addiction and then take positive steps to solve your problem. Go to self-help groups as well as to your doctor and friends. People can be very supportive if approached for help. If you don't, you could lose your friends, be demoted at work and find yourself at odds with your family.

Exercise

Enjoy yourself while exercising. If your body is exercised a lot, your whole personality will sparkle and your PSI powers will be sharpened and kept alert. Exercise freshens the mind and makes you feel good. Vigorous exercise will also help you relax more. Whatever form of exercise you undertake make sure you like it, otherwise you may give it up too quickly.

Aerobic exercises are in my opinion the most beneficial for your heart and lungs, blood circulation and general well-being. They could take the form of swimming, jogging, rowing, cycling (on an exercise bike or on the road), or vigorous dancing. I consider swimming to be the best of these. Even a skipping rope would be of use if you were confined to a hotel. I suggest that exercising this way for twenty minutes, three times a week would be sufficient for you to enjoy the rewards it will bring. The most important thing is to raise your heart rate to a target zone for your age. *Always consult a doctor before undertaking strenuous exercises*. Have your doctor work out a target zone for your heart rate.

You can enjoy exercises even in confined spaces like coaches and trains, or on aeroplanes. Lie back in your seat, relax, and then begin your exercises. Flex the muscles of each limb in turn. Start with your toes and work right up to your head. Flex your toes, your calf muscles, then your thigh muscles, relaxing them after each flexing. Continue upwards by flexing your posterior. Next, work on your stomach. Straighten your back and shoulders and spine and pull in your abdominal wall. Concentrate on your chest muscles and the muscles in your arms and then your neck. Stretch your whole body out as far as you can and relax again. Keep up these exercises for as long as you can.

Sleep: If you find it difficult to sleep, it may be because you have not had sufficient exercise or you are worried about an aspect of your life. We have already discussed blocking out your worries to enable you to sleep. If you find it difficult to concentrate or study, have a short sleep. Meditate and relax and tell yourself to have a fifteen to thirty minute nap. It will regenerate your whole system! Winston Churchill, the great statesman, was well-known for taking naps during the day. It enabled him to stay wide awake into the early hours of the morning when his opponents were exhausted.

Aggression: I used to be very irritable, always rushing about and flying off the handle if things did not go right. I realise now that much of it was to do with stress and wanting to succeed. Once I learned how to relax and use PSI powers to control my emotions I became a much happier and calmer person. Now, if I find myself running late for an appointment, I don't let it bother me. There is nothing I can do about it and I realise it is futile becoming emotionally upset.

Faith healers: Many wonderful 'cures' have taken place at Lourdes in France and with seventh sons of seventh sons and a number of psychic healers. I am wary of the claims of people with dubious backgrounds who charge for their healing. I do believe in the power of the mind and that it can heal the body and I do believe in natural healers. I have watched them at work. But there are also many charlatans in the world who make claims which a desperate person will believe as a last-resort cure. As it is usually the person's own faith and mind that cures these ailments I would try to effect a cure through traditional means and your own PSI power first.

Look at the way other races have controlled their bodies through mindpower. Fire dancers can actually walk across burning coals without feeling pain. People have psyched themselves to accept operations without anaesthetics and not felt pain. It can be done. Similarly, by willing the body to get better, patients have had what doctors will often describe as 'miracle' cures. Some doctors, I believe, are natural healers and while they may not realise this themselves, a look into their record will show a marvellous history of success with patients.

If you as a patient have a terminal disease and have tried every conventional method of healing, then I would not blame you for trying a last resort, even if the person offering help was of a doubtful reputation. It has been known that in cases like that, the patient will psych himself or herself into such a state of willingness to believe in a cure that a miracle will actually happen. Even though it was the patient's own PSI force that achieved this, it needed the catalyst from another party to spark it off.

If you need help, then you should go to a practitioner who you believe will do most to help you. If you prefer an osteopath, then go to one. If it is acupuncture you seek, then find a really good practitioner but be mindful that needles should be properly sterilised. Dirty needles is one of the ways of being infected with AIDS. Another thing to watch out for with AIDS is having medical treatment in primitive countries. Make sure that both doctors and dentists have sterilised their needles and other surgical equipment before you accept treatment. Don't be frightened or embarrassed to ask them what measures they have taken. It could save your life!

Music and healing: Music can have a great impact on our senses. It has the power to alter our mood and behaviour. It can unite people, make us happy or sad or calm our emotions. Successful musicians have a very strong sense of PSI and they can elicit or 'turn on' a mood through their inner creativeness. A London composer, Lawrence Ball, is convinced that PSI power has helped him to create music which is based on psychic 'sounds' to achieve a unity between the mind and body. His 'healing tone' tapes are now being used by some practitioners of the Alexander Technique which is widely acclaimed as an effective remedy for stress through relaxation and therapy. Lawrence found that his compositions achieved a psychic energy with a strong healing ethos which he was able to convey to students. Others have also adopted his music for movement therapy with mentally and physically handicapped people.

To sum up, this is my personal formula for health. I think you should follow me. But do check with your doctor to be sure.

1. No smoking.
2. Alcohol in moderation.
3. Fewer eggs, or none at all; although the white of eggs is alright.
4. No red meat.
5. Avoid foods with high animal fat content.
6. Eat lots of vegetables and fruit.
7. Also, complex carbohydrates for starch, bread, pasta and potatoes are fine in reasonable quantities. Avoid too much sugar.
8. Use vegetable oil in place of butter.
9. Exercise three times a week for twenty minutes a session.
10. If you are nervous or anxious allow yourself gently to unwind. You will be calmer – and healthier.

PSI and the cosmic forces

If we stretch our mental horizons and include the universe in our perception of things, we can embark on a fantastic voyage of new and exciting mind experiences. By opening the curtains to another dimension, we will also find that they have many practical applications in everyday life.

It is only recently that phenomena like black holes in space have received widespread prominence although astronomers have thought about them for years. People today are far more open to theories regarding different 'time zones' and 'timelessness' than they were in the past. The strictly defined rules of physics are being more closely questioned than before and the practice of astrology and numerology is no longer sneered at. And fewer people are willing to ridicule the theory, or phenomena, of communication with different life forms and other unexplained happenings which we will readily accept in Sci-fi movies and books.

How can that be of use on a practical level? Well, opening your mind and being receptive to new ideas and thoughts, will help you to adjust to an ever-changing world. You will not be regarded as being set in your ways and you should therefore be able to keep up with younger generations whose thought patterns might be more exciting or adventurous than the ones around which you developed. Being open-minded about new theories and ideas does not mean that you are required to believe them. If an idea is not acceptable at present, or seems outrageous in the context of our knowledge, we should still examine it carefully and scientifically and, if it does not make sense today, put it to one side for the future. Never reject anything outright. Remember the stubbornness of the 'flat-earthers' who refused to believe the world could be round.

In Chapter One of this book, I introduced a great author and philosopher of our time, Arthur Koestler. He and his devoted wife Cynthia, who at fifty-six was twenty-one years younger than her husband, killed themselves at their Knightsbridge flat in London in 1983, with an overdose of barbiturates and alcohol. Arthur, who was a friend of mine, had been suffering from poor health and wanted to avoid a painful death. We had known each other for some years and he became an absolute believer in life after death. He also expressed a great interest in reincarnation and wanted, in another life, or career, to have been a faith healer.

On several occasions, he intimated to me that it was partly as a result of my powers that he had decided to leave his money to create a chair in Parapsychology at a British university. He also talked to me about death and warned me on several occasions tha he would kill himself. He was not afraid of death in itself and regarded it as another passage. But he did fear the 'pain and humiliation' in the transition to death. He had completed most of his work on this planet and he was depressed with society and its beliefs. He felt he had another mission on another plane.

I did not think he would kill himself only six months after revealing his inner thoughts to me. His wife was relatively young and I would have thought she might have wanted to live longer. But they were

195

of the same mind. There was no question that she would stay on this planet and face life alone without him.

Because of his tremendous standing in British society, Arthur had access to many records of unexplained events which he was keen to publish to help promote a wider acceptance of PSI. Like many of us, Arthur had also experienced the effects of PSI power and the following story helped convince him of the existence of telepathy.

When he was fighting the Fascists in the Spanish Civil War, he was captured and thought he would be executed. At one point, believing that he was only hours from death, he cast his mind back to a book he had read and in particular, to a certain passage. '. . A passage in a novel by Thomas Mann called *Buddenbrooks*. In that passage Thomas Buddenbrooks, who knows that he is soon going to die, reads a little book which comforts him. Although the little book is not named in the novel I knew it was an essay on death by Schopenhauer.'

Arthur survived this ordeal and after he was released from prison, he wrote to Thomas Mann to say how much he had been comforted by his book. Mann had not read Schopenhauer's essay on death for forty years but for some unknown reason, he suddenly felt the urge to do so and was reaching for the essay at the same time as his front doorbell rang. It was the postman with Koestler's letter. Either Koestler had been able to communicate his thoughts telepathically, or Thomas Mann had precognition about the content of Koestler's letter. Whichever was so, it demonstrated the power of PSI.

Oxford University's Religious Experience Research Unit (RERU) opened its files for Koestler, adding yet more substantive proof of telepathy and

ESP. In one case, a father was desperately trying to console his distraught daughter who had been jilted for a second time. He could not find the words at first and then while getting her a drink he heard a voice say: 'As the sun sets, it also rises.' He repeated the words to his daughter and she quietened down. A year later his daughter was getting married and the reception was held at a very old country mansion. Inscribed in the old stone lintel over the door were the words: 'As the sun sets, it also rises.'

In another case – this one involved precognition – a man fell on to the underground railway line at the entrance to a London station just as a train appeared. Inside the train, and apparently for no known reason, a passenger suddenly pulled the emergency brake handle, prematurely stopping the train and thereby saving the man's life. The passenger had no way of knowing a man was on the line and the incident only came to light after the passenger was interviewed by London Transport police with a view to prosecuting him for stopping the train without reasonable grounds.

Arthur was also fascinated by the sixth sense in both animals and people and plants. The Russians had experimented with ESP in preparation of their space programme. One of the tests they had devised was to show the existence of ESP between mothers and babies. Mother rabbits were tested for their reaction when their offspring were killed thousands of miles away on a submarine. They registered a shock reaction at the precise time of death of their young.

Western and Eastern bloc agencies would love to use ESP-ionage. They have not dismissed the possibility of man being able to influence the course of missiles or alter important information in top security computers or read the minds of important people. The Kremlin's secret budget on mindpower experiments is estimated at around sixty-five million dollars whereas the Pentagon spends only a tenth of this.

Obviously I cannot say too much about this, but I have been asked to participate in several programmes of research involving strategic defence. I can however, tell you what has publicly been revealed about results of some of the tests. Other psychics like myself have been able to telepathically project their thoughts across thousands of miles to ships and aircraft and successfully give instructions to those in command. They have also been able to locate positions of missile bases, submarines and ships and 'see' inside top secret military bases.

Unfortunately, it is usually only well-known people with public credibility who are not ridiculed when they describe unusual happenings. American actress Shirley MacLaine had a premonition that something had happened to Peter Sellers shortly after he died. Lindsay Wagner, the actress who played Bionic Woman, was booked to fly out of Chicago with her mother on 25 May, 1979. She cancelled about ten minutes before boarding the aircraft because she had a terrible feeling that something was not right. The DC10 crashed killing more than two hundred and seventy passengers. Lindsay has also shown that she has precognition; when only fourteen years of age, she foresaw the house she would live in with her future husband.

TV star Erik Estrada was filming the hit series *Chips* when he was involved in a motorcycle accident that nearly killed him. If only he had listened to a warning from his mother, it might have been avoided. Carmen, his mother, had telephoned him three days earlier and told him that she had had a dream that he had visited her. She felt something was going to happen and told him to be careful when driving. Erik felt himself leaving his body after the accident but consciously thought to himself that he was too young to die.

The actress Rita Tushingham believes in communication with the dead through mediums. She was able to communicate with her sister who died when she was six months old. Peter Sellers' wife, Lynne Frederick, has made spiritual contact with the star on several occasions. A seance was held at the home of Michael Bentine, Sellers' friend, with a well-known medium. He told Lynne: 'I haven't really left you. Death is not the end.'

It is no coincidence that Lynne went to the home of Michael Bentine, a top British comedian. He is renowned for his psychic abilities. He foresaw the death of his son in a light aircraft twelve weeks before the accident happened. He told his son, who was called Gus, not to fly with his friend Andy as he had had a premonition that both boys would die in the plane. The warning was not heeded and the two young friends died instantly when their light plane crashed in the circumstances predicted by Michael.

The next day Michael felt a hand on his shoulder. It was his son Gus making a brief visitation to whisper the words: 'Daddy I'm terribly sorry – so sorry.' By a strange coincidence, Michael had predicted the death of other young airmen, but that was during the war. He had been an intelligence officer in the Air Force and was required to instruct crews. Occasionally, he would see the face of a young flier turn into a skull and would know that it would be the young man's last flight.

The former actor David Jannsen who starred in

Harry O, telephoned his favourite psychic after he foresaw his own death. In a dream, he saw himself being carried from his house after collapsing from a heart attack. Then he saw himself being buried. Two days later he had a massive heart attack and died.

I have already spoken of the tremendous PSI communication that exists between twins. This next story is a tragic illustration of that closeness. The case involved identical English twins called Joy and Margaret.

When the girls were four years old they were taken into care in Norfolk. Throughout their lives they had experienced each other's illnesses. Margaret, who had been twice married, had a job in Belgium, while her sister Joy had moved to Melbourne, Australia. In 1984, Joy who was on the other side of the world to her sister, suddenly developed a blinding headache within hours of her sister's death. She experienced pain for three days as well as a growing sense of doom for Margaret. Then finally, an explanation was given. News reached the family that Margaret had been found dead in a Belgian wood. She had been shot ten times in the head.

Barbara Woodhouse, who is world-famous for the way she treats animals and gets the best out of them, uses her PSI powers in other ways as well. She can contact people without using conventional means of telecommunication. Her son was at Wimbledon watching tennis when a company rang offering a job interview. He wanted that position badly and Barbara sent him a telepathic message to phone home. He did so within ten minutes. Barbara complains that electrical gadgets often stop working in her presence and she also has a tame but mischievous ghost at her home in Hertfordshire.

A positive PSI practised by English actress Diane Langton has, she says, brought her health, wealth and happiness. She calls her positive thoughts 'psycho-pictography.' When she was still trying to make it as an actress, she lived in a crummy flat without a bathroom but visualised a beautiful house with a swimming-pool. Now she owns one just like she visualised it would be. She describes her PSI thoughts in the following way: 'I do it every day, usually as soon as I wake up in the morning: I picture myself in somewhere like the Wembley Stadium and I am singing to thousands. I can hear the applause. If I wanted a Rolls Royce, I would picture it in my driveway and I would get it.'

When she wanted a separation from her first husband, he refused to go away and pestered her. To achieve a final split, she visualised him waving goodbye and leaving her and the problem soon came to an end.

Ghost stories are very much part of our tradition and folk lore, but try telling a friend you have seen a ghost and watch the reaction. Will it be one of incredulity or will your friend think you have finally flipped your lid? Members of the *Dallas* cast, including actress Linda Gray and Patrick Duffy, were spooked out when they saw the apparition of actor Jim Davis who played Jock Ewing. He began haunting the set in a friendly way soon after his death.

There have been hundreds of sightings of ghosts in castles and old homes. The royal family is convinced of the presence of ghosts in several properties owned by them. The Roman author Pliny, who was regarded as a reliable and accurate historian of his times, told the story of waiting one night in a haunted house and following a ghost which, with much rattling of chains, disappeared at a certain spot. He marked the spot where the apparition had disappeared and the next day ordered a dig. A slave had been buried at the spot and after the remains had received a proper burial, it no longer haunted the house.

An English psychiatrist, Dr R Kenneth McAll, has claimed an amazing success curing patients through dead 'spirits.' His theory was that many women were extremely unsettled over abortions and would, even years later, suffer because of the ghosts of their dead children. He would lay those ghosts to rest after exorcising the patient, with whom he would then pray for forgiveness. He said that hidden guilt in a patient's ancestors can also be the cause for a person's abnormal behaviour.

Faith in divine providence brought its rewards to one remarkable man. He was a medical missionary in China and was held for four years as a prisoner in a Japanese war camp. While there he had a vision of Christ joining him and giving him guidance. On his return to Britain, he sought divine help to buy a house and was led to a twenty-eight room mansion dating back to Saxon and Roman times and formerly owned by the famous Sherlock Holmes writer, Sir Arthur Conan Doyle. He did not have the money to buy it although he desperately wanted it. His faith got him his wish: a patient bought him the house together with valuable Chinese pottery sets from the Ming Dynasty period. Soon after he moved in, the writer's ghost appeared and Dr McAll exorcised this spirit.

Dr McAll was also asked to exorcise underground buildings in the British Channel Islands in which Nazi labour camp prisoners had been made to work. Some had died or had been killed and thrown into the concrete constructions. These unhappy souls were not properly laid to rest and had haunted the place since, the psychiatrist claimed.

I have known a number of people who have related their near death experiences to me. Studies have also been conducted into this subject and the results have been of some comfort to those who feel they are shortly to share this experience. From what has been told by those entering this different state, it is difficult not to believe that there is life hereafter.

The majority of near death experiences related to me, have been pleasant. The 'victims' have felt at peace with the world and happy in their state, almost a euphoric happiness. Some entered dark tunnels and after being pulled through them, found a new and delicious floating existence in which there was a dazzling, but not a blinding, light. Others talked about an out of body experience and had been in two minds about leaving it permanently or returning to it. A final stage of 'knowing' was reached by few. The knowing stage was one of completeness, harmony and communication with others which was then shattered on the subject's 'return.'

Nature, numerology, and cosmic forces

Plant life responds favourably to PSI power. I personally talk to my favourite plants and stroke them and urge them to grow. Tests have been done which prove that the response to this kind of treatment is highly beneficial and plants which have not been given the same doting attention have not fared so well. Electrodes attached to plants have registered changes when the plants received 'emotional' shocks. In one test, live prawns were dropped into boiling water and registered 'anxiety' as a result.

The famous Findhorn Community in Scotland, which has attracted people from all over the world and was started by a former Air Force squadron leader, Peter Caddy, had enormous success with growing plants and vegetables in 'hostile' soil. The community was told that their windswept landscape at Findhorn bay overlooking the Firth of Moray would support very little apart from natural weed. Within a short time, the community was growing record size vegetables which attracted global interest. The greatest input, according to the community, was PSI power. They will their crops to grow! Human development has also progressed rapidly over the years at Findhorn. Certain members of the community found they were receiving, and could send, telepathic messages from inmates of slave labour camps in Russia.

Numerology: Ancient civilisations were aware of the importance of numbers as much as we are today. But then, numerology had a mystical importance as well, sometimes involving magic and philosophy as in the Hebrew Kabala. And it has always been linked to fate through astrology, Tarot cards, I Ching, Rune stones and the casting of die. Planets and the laws of physics and mathematics are dependent on numerology. From gambling to providing estimates for work, we too are dependent on numbers and mathematical equations.

PSI and numerology: Use your PSI power to make numbers bring you good luck! We all have our favourite numbers. Use them positively to make things happen for you. By using positive PSI power and reinforcing your positiveness when your lucky number comes up, you will automatically increase your chances of success. Numerology itself does not involve ESP. It is the art of reading character and personalty through numbers, usually between 1 and 9. Your birth number, for example, is arrived at by adding up all the digits of your birth date and then reducing them to a single number between 1 and 9. If you were born on the 1 December, 1968, (1.12.1968), you would calculate your birth number in the following way:

$$1+1+2+1+9+6+8=28 \quad 2+8=10 \quad 1+0=1$$

So if you were born then, your birth number is 1. Ancient Greek philosophers like Pythagoras attached supreme importance to numbers, giving them specific meanings which have since been broadened and adapted. Pythagoras said: 'All things are numbers.' They were the first things in the 'whole of nature.' Heaven was a musical scale and a number. Numbers constituted the essence of things.

More complicated character assessments can be made by determining your number, and for this you must first convert your name into figures in the following way:

1	2	3	4	5	6	7	8	9
A	B	C	D	E	F	G	H	I
J	K	L	M	N	O	P	Q	R
S	T	U	V	W	X	Y	Z	

Convert each letter of your name to a digit and then add them up and reduce them as with the birth number until you have a single digit number. If your name is Jo Smith, your name number would be:

$$1+6+1+4+9+2+8=31 \quad 3+1=4$$

Jo Smith has a name number of 4.

Interpreting your number: The following attributes have been attached to the numbers 1–9:

1: Independence, leadership, ambition, confidence.
2: Compatibility, balance, harmony, diplomacy.
3: Creativity, freedom of thought, independence.
4: Industriousness, soundness, dependability.
5: Daring, brave, adventurous, free.
6: Responsibility, peace, harmony, leadership.
7: Mind development, mystery, wisdom, understanding.
8: Material and financial success, authority, balance.
9: Achievement, vision, power, supremacy.

Your birth or name number could be quite different from your 'favourite' or 'lucky' number. My 'lucky' numbers are 11, 7, and 17. I have won a lot of raffles by choosing the number 11. My son was born at eleven pm and a lot of my friends find 11 a significant number. Numbers can also be closely linked to your destiny, as they were in the case of John Lennon.

John's special number was 9. He was born on 9 October, 1940 and he was spotted by Brian Epstein at the Cavern in Liverpool on 9 November, 1961. The following year the Beatles first record contract was signed on 9 May and their first record *Love Me Do* was on Parlophone R4949. John met Yoko on 9 November, 1966. At the time she was living on West 72nd (7+2=9) Street, New York. As a boy, John would travel on the 72 bus to his art college, and his songs included *Re-*

volution 9, Number 9 Dream and *One After 909*. (He wrote this last song at his mother's home in 9 Newcastle Road, Liverpool.) When he was shot outside his New York apartment, John Lennon's body was taken to Roosevelt Hospital on Ninth Avenue.

Gambling and PSI: Gambling involves luck and the element of chance which can be calculated by numbers. Before you set off to the racetrack or betting shop and test your lucky number, stop and think on a practical PSI level. Ask yourself this question: 'Who's richer – me or the bookies?' If you are not richer, I would advise that you do not gamble away your hard-earned money. The odds are on their side. It's their business and when it comes to betting the odds are that they will out-psych you every day and every way. If you are so rich that losing won't affect you, have a light-hearted flutter but don't become obsessed with gambling, it can be a very costly and dangerous disease.

How much of a gambler are you? Try this quiz answering each question with either a 'Yes,' 'No' or 'Not sure.'

1. Do you live in constant hope of winning the pools?
2. Do you have ready formed plans on how to spend the money?
3. Do you purchase tickets for lotteries?
4. Is watching the racing on TV much more fun if you have money at stake?
5. Is the logic of winning a fortune for a small stake appealing to you?
6. Do you find the atmosphere of a casino exhilarating?
7. Do you always bet on the biggest horse race event of the year?

8. Do you ever bet on the outcome of a friendly game of sport, say tennis?
9. Would you place a bet on a horse if its name or something about it appealed to you?
10. Do you ever have small bets with colleagues at work?
11. Do you think you could be lucky at gambling?
12. Would you be among the last to go home in a late night card session with friends?
13. Do you get a thrill from winning?
14. If you were offered the choice of playing a game for money or playing on a friendly basis, would you choose the former?
15. Given the opportunity, would you prefer a game of poker with friends to going to the theatre?

Scoring: Score two points for every 'Yes' answer, one point for 'Not sure,' and 0 for 'No.'

A score of 26 or more suggests you might have a problem and it could be a good idea to pay a visit to Gamblers Anonymous. I suggest you do not go to Las Vegas or Atlantic City. There are some very rich casino groups in those towns and they would love to entertain you while you still had some money left.

A score of 12 or over indicates that you are at least predisposed to be the gambling type. In personality theory, this means you are more sensitive to reward than punishment. A score of 18 or more suggests a definite leaning towards being a gambler. If you can control this instinct you could do well in business because you are also a positive personality.

I do not like to gamble because of some bad experiences in the past but nevertheless I would still use my PSI powers if the gambling urge possessed me. I'll tell you what I did in my more foolish moments: Shipi and I made a lot of money gambling one night in a London casino and the following day I felt nauseated by the fact that I had used my powers wrongly. It affected me so much that I felt I was going to die. In the end I threw away the money – about thirty thousand dollars and felt instant relief. After that I swore I would work hard for my money.

My method of gambling was the following: I tried to use my mind to control the ball in a game of roulette. But first, I would stand in an uncrowded spot and just watch and see which way the game was going. I would then relax and begin to concentrate on the ball and visualise it appearing on certain numbers. Without placing money on the board, I would see how many times I could get it right. If it worked every time I would then start putting money on the game and back my judgment.

I would only place the money on the table after the croupier turned the wheel; that way I felt I had better control. I would never take my eyes off the ball and with the help of mindpower, I would will it to fall on a particular number. I also made sure that another person was not trying to do the same thing at my table, as otherwise there could be a psychic clash. But I can promise you that the best and most satisfactory way to a fortune is still through hard work, making use of your PSI power, and positive thought!

PSI power and the positive principle

You are now ready to test if your personality is compatible with psychic powers. I suspect it is. By the very fact that you have read this book and taken the trouble to do the tests, you have already shown a positive attitude in your thinking and you are on the brink of changing your life style for the better. After the test, I will go over some of the positive principles you will need in situations that are likely to arise in your life.

The PSI power compatibility test: Answer each question with either 'Yes,' 'Not sure,' or 'No.'

1. Do you often feel bored?
2. Do other people consider you a lively individual?
3. Do you prefer to have a lot going on around you?
4. Do you ever imitate your boss at work?
5. Do you ever pretend you are someone else on the telephone?
6. Do you ever play a trick at somebody else's expense?
7. Are you good at thinking of a quick reply when asked questions?
8. Do you find it hard to arrive for appointments on time?
9. Do you prefer talking to reading?

10. Do you often interrupt when others are talking?
11. Do you sometimes wear outrageous clothes?
12. Do you sometimes tend to get carried away and overdo things?
13. Are you good at telling jokes?
14. Can you be the life and soul of a party?
15. Are you often introducing people to one another?
16. Do you find it hard to refuse people?
17. Do you tend to overlook small details?
18. Are you sometimes careless with money?
19. Do you prefer going out to watching television?
20. Do you enjoy talking to strangers on holiday?
21. Are you in the habit of offering help to other people?
22. Do you tend to believe in astrological predictions when they are in your favour?
23. Do you tend to disbelieve predictions if they are not favourable?
24. Do you enjoy watching soap operas on television?
25. In most situations, would you rather talk than listen?
26. Are you the type that speaks what is on your mind?
27. Are you quick to give an opinion when with a group of people?
28. Do you tend to tell 'white' lies?
29. Do you try and ignore minor illnesses?
30. Do you tend to give others a second chance?

Scoring: Give yourself 2 points for every 'Yes' answer, 1 point for 'Not sure,' and 0 for 'No.'

How did you fare? A score of 36 or more means

you are the impulsive, outgoing, social type. You seek stimulation and excitement and one of the ways you achieve this is through being a sociable and fun person. You also have strong psychic abilities which you can further develop by allowing your mind to absorb psychic messages which it can easily do.

A score of 35 or less suggests your basic character is more introverted and you tend to be a quieter, more home orientated person. You consider your opinions carefully and you may have a very keen intellect. Your PSI powers are certainly present and the potential to develop them is enormous because of your capacity for inner thought.

The positive path

PSI meditation and relaxation: This is the first and most important step you must take before attempting to use your PSI power. Whatever the situation, you must learn to relax your body and your mind before you begin using the tremendous PSI energy you are capable of producing. Once you have mastered this, you will be able to control your emotions and your body at the most trying periods of your life. You will also be able to rest your mind on command, thus restoring energy that has been drained. Controlling your mind also means that you will be able to look at problems from the outside – as if you were a third party. Everone is capable of relaxation and concentration. Practise this constantly. You will be amazed at the results!

Use your powers: Do not waste your very special powers. They *are* there. They may not always be apparent but you do have them. Work at everything I have suggested and you will soon find yourself doing a better job and enjoying yourself more.

Communication: I cannot emphasise enough the need to master this thoroughly. It is one of the most important gifts of life bringing huge rewards to those who excel at it.

Think positive: Believe in anything strongly enough and there is every chance you will get it. Use this power with all the other gifts you possess and you will make a success of life.

Love relationships: Psych your boyfriend or girlfriend, wife or partner, with everything you have learned. Play love games with your partner and you will find yourself irresistible to the opposite sex. Believe in your own attractiveness.

Think big: Don't be frightened by your bank manager or boss. You are as important, if not more, than your boss or manager. Eventually you will overtake their position. They are there to serve your needs as well. Don't be bullied by them. Stand up for yourself. Don't be afraid of making decisions.

Health: Look after your body. Exercise it daily and don't abuse it. Play sports you enjoy. Try to squeeze in those aerobic exercises three times a week and push yourself for twenty minutes in each of those sessions. Don't fall prey to sickness. Banish it. Tell it to go away. Fight illness with positive PSI power.

Personal problems: Don't let them get on top of you. It is not worth making yourself ill or stressful over somebody else. They will only enjoy the power they have over you. Be firm. If you have money problems, don't give up. Work out a system to beat your bad debts. Ask your bank for help. Face up to problems otherwise you will never overcome them.

Wealth: You can be rich if you set your mind to it. Read about others who have become millionaires despite all odds. Tell yourself that you can do it too. Set goals, small ones at first, and then bigger ones until you make a practice of success. Tell yourself that you will soon achieve success and that it is only a matter of time. Believe in yourself and others will soon believe in you.

Happiness: This takes priority over everything. Achieve this and most other things will come your way. Psych yourself to happiness. If you are unhappy, find out why. Look at yourself from outside of yourself. Communicate with others who are important to you. Alter your life style so you achieve the things you want. You can do it. Believe it.

Psych yourself with positives: Make a list each day of the positives you wish to achieve. Write down your name and your objectives. Here are a few examples:

I (name) am going to stand up for my rights.
I (name) will finish the job no matter what.
I (name) know I am attractive/lovely and will be liked.
I (name) will beat this disease.
I (name) will win the next time I play with my opponent.
I (name) will not let the boss get me down.

I (name) will book the holiday I want.
I (name) know I will not catch my partner's cold.
I (name) will not let the past worry me.

Now you are ready to embark on a new stage of your life. You have the positive power of achieving anything you want. Others have done it before you. Health, wealth and happiness is yours for the taking. You have a wonderful opportunity of experimenting and entering new territories with your mind. How well you do that depends on *your* application and approach. I wish you luck on this exciting journey. If you enjoy the ride, tell others. Share your happiness with friends like I have shared mine with you! Go for it and Bon Voyage!